ADVANCED DUNGEONS & DYNAMICS 365 IMPLEMENTATION GUIDE

THE WATERDEEP TRADING COMPANY PROJECT

MODULE 5: CONFIGURING VENDORS AND PURCHASING PRODUCTS

MURRAY FIFE

ISBN-13: 978-1077211551

Preface

I have been reviving an old project that started a while ago and have started up a new project blog to track the progress. Being a lifelong fan of Dungeons & Dragons, with the unfortunate problem that I cannot find anyone to play with I have decided to create a test implementation Dynamics 365 in the AD&D format just to see how it would work and if I can find some creative ways to use Dynamics 365 and chose to implement the **Waterdeep Trading Company** as an example where I can track their many legal (and not so legal) entities within Faerûn.

dync
www.dynamicscompanions.com
Dynamics Companions

- 3 -

www.blindsquirrelpublishing.com
© 2019 Blind Squirrel Publishing, LLC , All Rights Reserved

BLIND SQUIRREL
PUBLISHING

Table of Contents

dync
www.dynamicscompanions.com
Dynamics Companions

- 5 -

www.blindsquirrelpublishing.com
© 2019 Blind Squirrel Publishing, LLC , All Rights Reserved

BLIND SQUIRREL
PUBLISHING

Introduction

Now that we have our inventory configured and we have set up our products, we can start stocking our inventory in the **Waterdeep Trading Company Store**.

These products don't fall off the back of a cart and magically appear for free though (not usually), so we will need to start procuring our new stock the old fashioned way by buying it from the dealers and traders within **Waterdeep**.

In this module, we will show you how to set up the procurement system and start buying and receiving products into the store.

Topics Covered

- Configuring the Purchasing Controls and Profiles

- Creating Vendor Profiles

- Purchasing Products

Configuring the Purchasing Controls and Profiles

Before we start buying any products though, there are some small configurations that we need to make to the purchasing system that we will need to do to ensure that the inventory is tracked correctly within the system.

Topics Covered

- Updating the Item Groups with default Posting Accounts

- Creating a Posting Profile

- Configuring the default Posting Profile

Updating the Item Groups with default Posting Accounts

The first thing that we will want to do is to update the Item Groups that we configured earlier to have some default accounts that we will post to when we receive our inventory through the purchasing system.

If we don't have these configured, then the system will balk a little. So let's set these up now and save a little heartburn later on.

Topics Covered

- Opening the Item Groups form
- Updating the default posting accounts

Opening the Item Groups form

To do this we will need to return to the **Item groups** maintenance form.

How to do it...

Step 1: Open the Item groups form through the menu search

We can find the **Item groups** form through the menu search feature.

We can do this by clicking on the search icon in the header of the form (or by pressing **ALT+G**)

and then type in **item gr** into the search box. Then you will be able to select the **Item groups** form from the dropdown list.

This will open up the **Item groups** maintenance form with the item groups that we have already configured and linked to the products in the system.

dyn**c**
dynamics companions

www.dynamicscompanions.com
Dynamics Companions

- 10 -

www.blindsquirrelpublishing.com
© 2019 Blind Squirrel Publishing, LLC , All Rights Reserved

BLIND SQUIRREL
PUBLISHING

Opening the Item Groups form

How to do it...

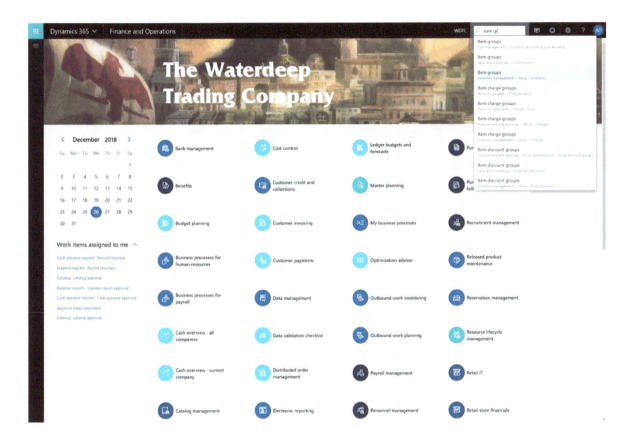

Step 1: Open the Item groups form through the menu search

We can find the **Item groups** form through the menu search feature.

We can do this by clicking on the search icon in the header of the form (or by pressing **ALT+G**) and then type in **item gr** into the search box. Then you will be able to select the **Item groups** form from the dropdown list.

dync
Dynamics Companions

www.dynamicscompanions.com
Dynamics Companions

- 11 -

www.blindsquirrelpublishing.com
© 2019 Blind Squirrel Publishing, LLC , All Rights Reserved

BLIND SQUIRREL
PUBLISHING

Opening the Item Groups form

How to do it...

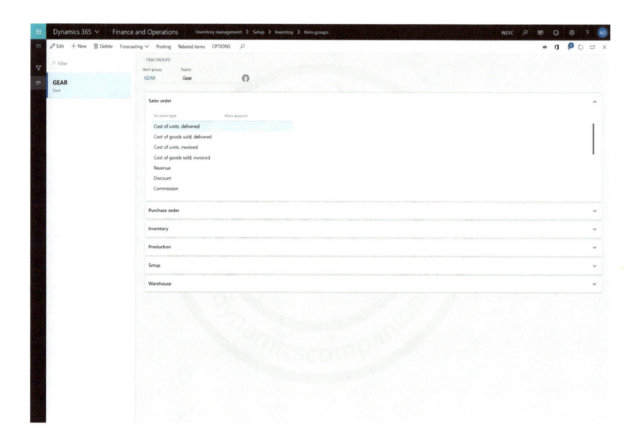

Step 1: Open the Item groups form through the menu search

This will open up the **Item groups** maintenance form with the item groups that we have already configured and linked to the products in the system.

dynʗc
dynamics companions

www.dynamicscompanions.com
Dynamics Companions

- 12 -

www.blindsquirrelpublishing.com
© 2019 Blind Squirrel Publishing, LLC , All Rights Reserved

BLIND SQUIRREL
PUBLISHING

Updating the default posting accounts

Now we will want to update a few of the default posting accounts in the Item groups.

How to do it...

Step 1: Click on the Edit button

To start off, we will want to switch to the edit mode within the record view.

To do this just click on the **Edit** button.

This will allow us to change the default **Main accounts** associated with the account types.

Step 2: Expand Purchase order tab

We will want to change the **Purchase order** accounts right now, so

To do this, all we need to do is expand the **Purchase order** tab.

Step 3: Select the Cost of purchased materials received (Main account)

We will start by assigning the main account to the Cost of purchased materials received the main account.

To do this, we will just need to pick the **Cost of purchased materials received (Main account)** option from the dropdown list.

This time, we will want to click on the **Cost of purchased materials received (Main account)** dropdown list and pick **1330 (INV - Finished Goods)**.

Step 4: Choose the Purchase expenditure uninvoiced (Main account)

Next, we will want to assign a default account for the un-invoiced purchases.

To do this just pick the **Purchase expenditure uninvoiced (Main account)** option from the dropdown list.

This time, we will want to click on the **Purchase expenditure uninvoiced (Main account)** dropdown list and select **1330 (INV - Unbilled Costs & Fees)**.

Step 5: Update the Purchase accrual (Main account)

Finally, we will want to add a default account for the purchase accruals.

To do this, we will just need to change the **Purchase accrual (Main account)** value.

This time, we will want to set the **Purchase accrual (Main account)** to **1330 (INV - Unbilled Costs & Fees)**.

Step 6: Click on the Save button

After we have done that we can save the Item group changes.

To do this, all we need to do is click on the **Save** button.

Updating the default posting accounts

How to do it...

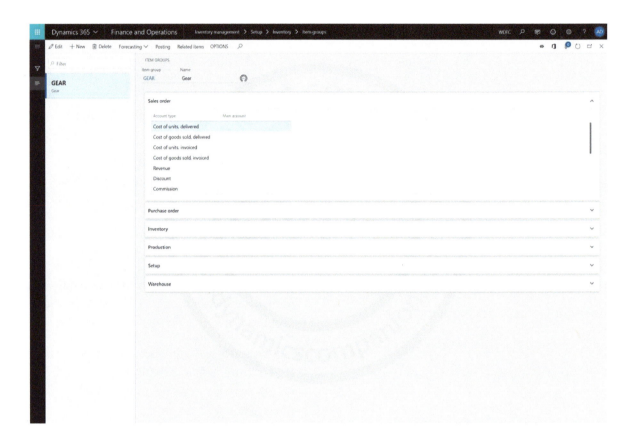

Step 1: Click on the Edit button

To start off, we will want to switch to the edit mode within the record view.

To do this just click on the **Edit** button.

Updating the default posting accounts

How to do it...

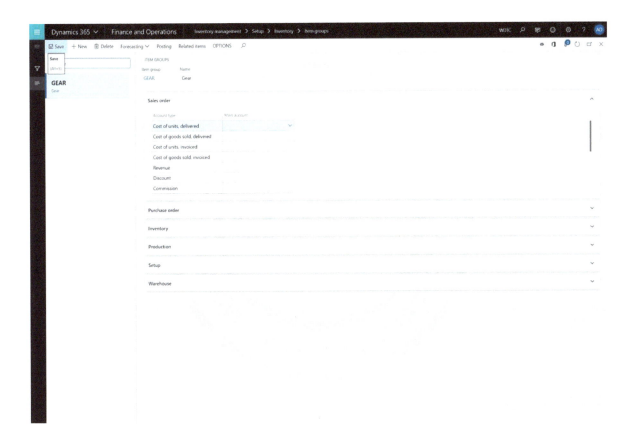

Step 1: Click on the Edit button

This will allow us to change the default **Main accounts** associated with the account types.

dync
www.dynamicscompanions.com
Dynamics Companions

- 15 -

www.blindsquirrelpublishing.com
© 2019 Blind Squirrel Publishing, LLC, All Rights Reserved

BLIND SQUIRREL
PUBLISHING

Updating the default posting accounts

How to do it...

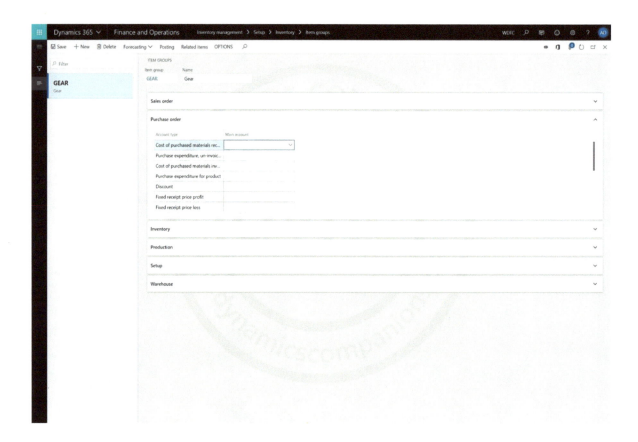

Step 2: Expand Purchase order tab

We will want to change the **Purchase order** accounts right now, so

To do this, all we need to do is expand the **Purchase order** tab.

Updating the default posting accounts

How to do it...

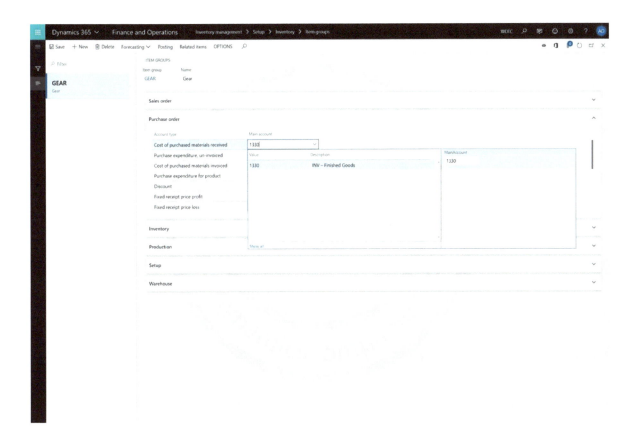

Step 3: Select the Cost of purchased materials received (Main account)

We will start by assigning the main account to the Cost of purchased materials received the main account.

To do this, we will just need to pick the **Cost of purchased materials received (Main account)** option from the dropdown list.

This time, we will want to click on the **Cost of purchased materials received (Main account)** dropdown list and pick **1330 (INV - Finished Goods)**.

Updating the default posting accounts

How to do it...

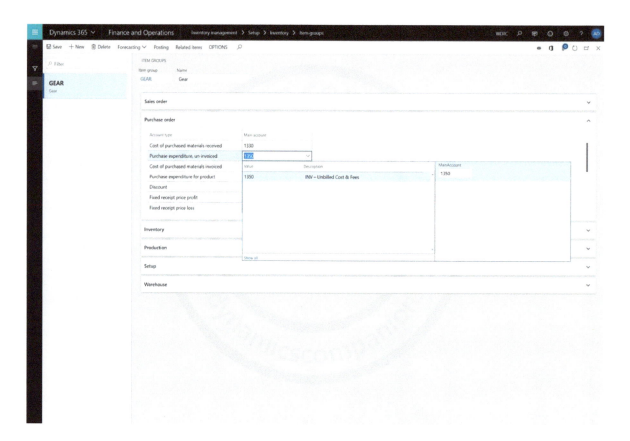

Step 4: Choose the Purchase expenditure uninvoiced (Main account)

Next, we will want to assign a default account for the un-invoiced purchases.

To do this just pick the **Purchase expenditure uninvoiced (Main account)** option from the dropdown list.

This time, we will want to click on the **Purchase expenditure uninvoiced (Main account)** dropdown list and select **1330 (INV - Unbilled Costs & Fees)**.

dync
dynamics companions

www.dynamicscompanions.com
Dynamics Companions

- 18 -

www.blindsquirrelpublishing.com
© 2019 Blind Squirrel Publishing, LLC , All Rights Reserved

BLIND SQUIRREL
PUBLISHING

Updating the default posting accounts

How to do it...

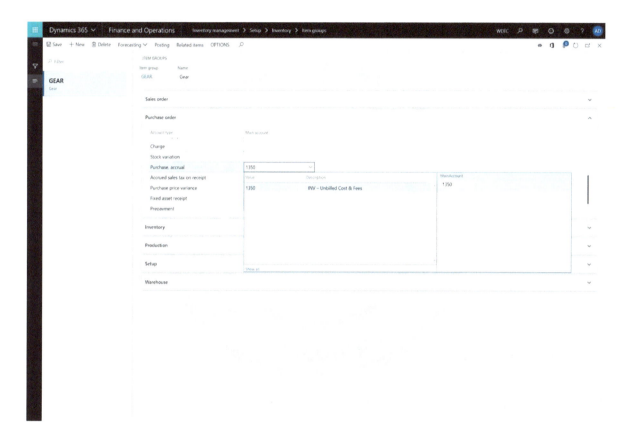

Step 5: Update the Purchase accrual (Main account)

Finally, we will want to add a default account for the purchase accruals.

To do this, we will just need to change the **Purchase accrual (Main account)** value.

This time, we will want to set the **Purchase accrual (Main account)** to **1330 (INV - Unbilled Costs & Fees)**.

www.dynamicscompanions.com
Dynamics Companions

- 19 -

www.blindsquirrelpublishing.com
© 2019 Blind Squirrel Publishing, LLC , All Rights Reserved

BLIND SQUIRREL
PUBLISHING

Updating the default posting accounts

How to do it...

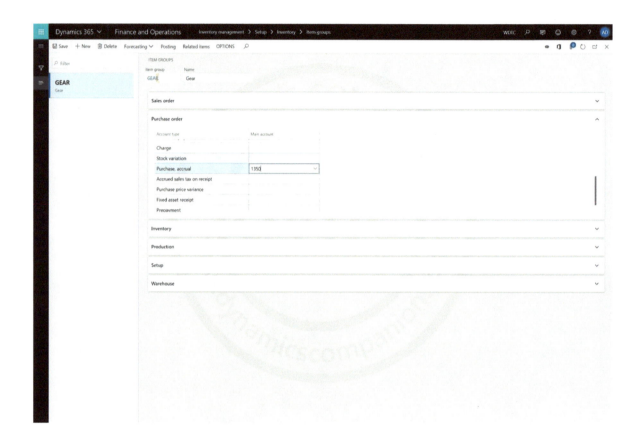

Step 6: Click on the Save button

After we have done that we can save the Item group changes.

To do this, all we need to do is click on the **Save** button.

dync
www.dynamicscompanions.com
Dynamics Companions

- 20 -

www.blindsquirrelpublishing.com
© 2019 Blind Squirrel Publishing, LLC , All Rights Reserved

BLIND SQUIRREL
PUBLISHING

Review

That wasn't hard was it. Now when we start receiving our newly purchased products, the system will know where to post the transactions within the ledger.

www.dynamicscompanions.com
Dynamics Companions

- 21 -

www.blindsquirrelpublishing.com
© 2019 Blind Squirrel Publishing, LLC , All Rights Reserved

BLIND SQUIRREL
PUBLISHING

Creating a Posting Profile

Next we will want to configure a default **Posting profile** which will be used by Dynamics 365 to default in some of the other Purchasing account defaults.

Topics Covered

- Opening the Vendor posting profiles form

- Creating a General Vendor Posting Profile

Opening the Vendor posting profiles form

To do this we will first need to open up the **Vendor posting profiles** maintenance form.

How to do it...

Step 1: Open the Vendor posting profiles form through the menu search

We can find the **Vendor posting profiles** form through the menu search feature.

We can do this by clicking on the search icon in the header of the form (or by pressing **ALT+G**)

and then type in **vendor p pr** into the search box. Then you will be able to select the **Vendor posting profiles** form from the dropdown list.

This will open up the **Vendor posting profiles** maintenance page where we will be able to set up our new default posting profile.

Opening the Vendor posting profiles form

How to do it...

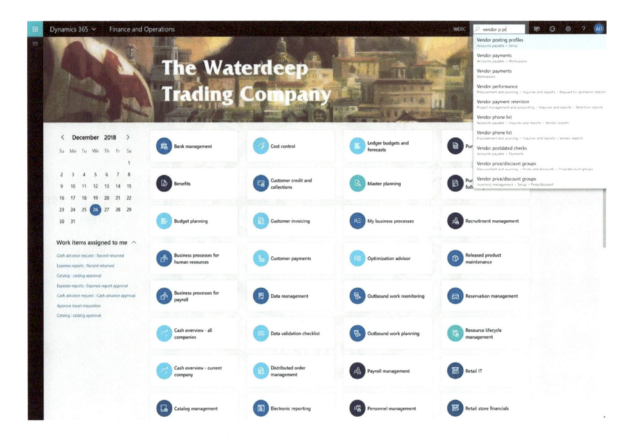

Step 1: Open the Vendor posting profiles form through the menu search

We can find the **Vendor posting profiles** form through the menu search feature.

We can do this by clicking on the search icon in the header of the form (or by pressing **ALT+G**) and then type in **vendor p pr** into the search box. Then you will be able to select the **Vendor posting profiles** form from the dropdown list.

dync
www.dynamicscompanions.com
Dynamics Companions

- 24 -

www.blindsquirrelpublishing.com
© 2019 Blind Squirrel Publishing, LLC , All Rights Reserved

BLIND SQUIRREL
PUBLISHING

Opening the Vendor posting profiles form

How to do it...

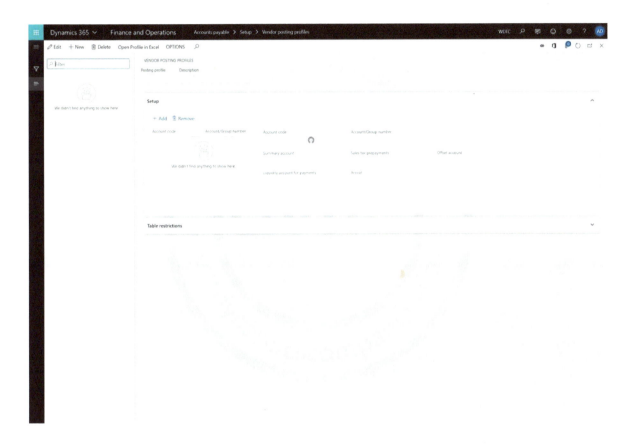

Step 1: Open the Vendor posting profiles form through the menu search

This will open up the **Vendor posting profiles** maintenance page where we will be able to set up our new default posting profile.

dync
dynamics companions

www.dynamicscompanions.com
Dynamics Companions

- 25 -

www.blindsquirrelpublishing.com
© 2019 Blind Squirrel Publishing, LLC , All Rights Reserved

BLIND SQUIRREL
PUBLISHING

Creating a General Vendor Posting Profile

Now that we are in the right place we can move on and set up a General posting profile.

How to do it...

Step 1: Click on the New button

We will start off by creating a new **Vendor posting profile** record.

To do this just click on the **New** button.

Step 2: Update the Posting profile

We will now want to assign the new Posting profile a code that we will use to reference it.

To do this just change the **Posting profile** value.

For this example, we will want to set the **Posting profile** to **GENERAL**.

Step 3: Update the Description

And then we will want to give the posting profile a better description to accompany the code.

To do this, we will just need to change the **Description** value.

This time, we will want to set the **Description** to **General Posting Profile**.

Step 4: Click on the Add button

Now we will want to add a posting profile that is to be used for all vendors.

To do this just click on the **Add** button.

Step 5: Select the Account code

Since this will apply to all of the vendors, we want to change the select to be all vendors.

To do this just select the **Account code** option from the dropdown list.

This time, we will want to click on the **Account code** dropdown list and select **All**.

Step 6: Choose the Summary Account

Now we will specify that the summary account for the vendors will be the A/P Trade account.

To do this, we will just need to select the **Summary Account** option from the dropdown list.

For this example, we will want to click on the **Summary Account** dropdown list and pick **2110 (A/P Trade)**.

Step 7: Select the Liquidity account for payments

And then we will want to specify that the payment will be posted to the cash account in the ledger.

To do this we will just need to pick the **Liquidity account for payments** option from the dropdown list.

This time, we will want to click on the **Liquidity account for payments** dropdown list and pick **1010 (CASH Operating Account)**.

Step 8: Click on the Save button

After we have done that we can save the posting profile and we are done.

To do this just click on the **Save** button.

Creating a General Vendor Posting Profile

How to do it...

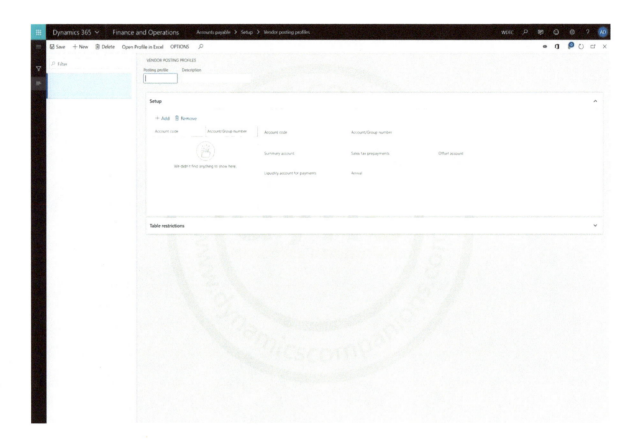

Step 1: Click on the New button

We will start off by creating a new **Vendor posting profile** record.

To do this just click on the **New** button.

dync
www.dynamicscompanions.com
Dynamics Companions

- 28 -

www.blindsquirrelpublishing.com
© 2019 Blind Squirrel Publishing, LLC , All Rights Reserved

BLIND SQUIRREL
PUBLISHING

Creating a General Vendor Posting Profile

How to do it...

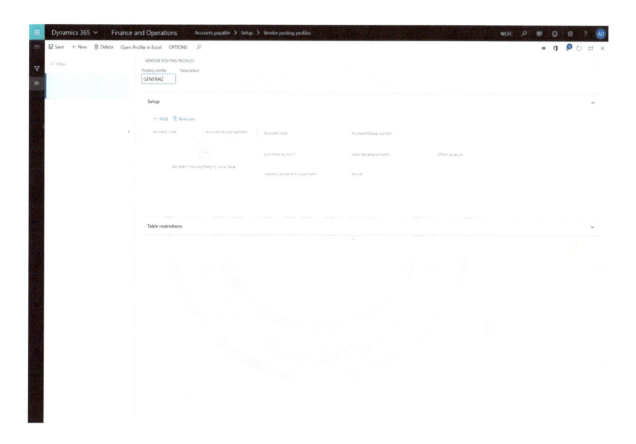

Step 2: Update the Posting profile

We will now want to assign the new Posting profile a code that we will use to reference it.

To do this just change the **Posting profile** value.

For this example, we will want to set the **Posting profile** to **GENERAL**.

Creating a General Vendor Posting Profile

How to do it...

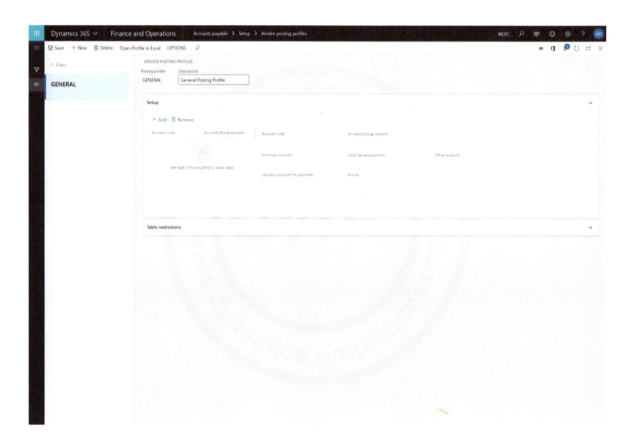

Step 3: Update the Description

And then we will want to give the posting profile a better description to accompany the code.

To do this, we will just need to change the **Description** value.

This time, we will want to set the **Description** to **General Posting Profile**.

dync
dynamics companions

www.dynamicscompanions.com
Dynamics Companions

- 30 -

www.blindsquirrelpublishing.com
© 2019 Blind Squirrel Publishing, LLC , All Rights Reserved

BLIND SQUIRREL
PUBLISHING

Creating a General Vendor Posting Profile

How to do it...

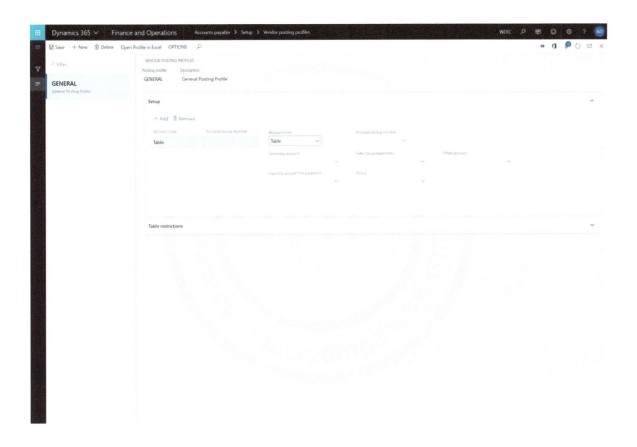

Step 4: Click on the Add button

Now we will want to add a posting profile that is to be used for all vendors.

To do this just click on the **Add** button.

dync
www.dynamicscompanions.com
Dynamics Companions

- 31 -

www.blindsquirrelpublishing.com
© 2019 Blind Squirrel Publishing, LLC , All Rights Reserved

BLIND SQUIRREL
PUBLISHING

Creating a General Vendor Posting Profile

How to do it...

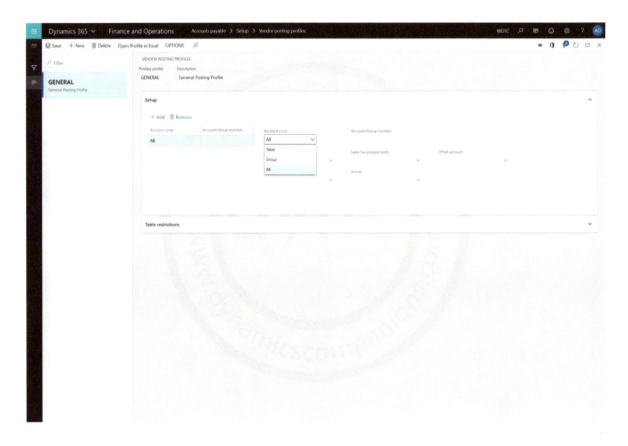

Step 5: Select the Account code

Since this will apply to all of the vendors, we want to change the select to be all vendors.

To do this just select the **Account code** option from the dropdown list.

This time, we will want to click on the **Account code** dropdown list and select **All**.

www.dynamicscompanions.com
Dynamics Companions

- 32 -

www.blindsquirrelpublishing.com
© 2019 Blind Squirrel Publishing, LLC , All Rights Reserved

BLIND SQUIRREL
PUBLISHING

Creating a General Vendor Posting Profile

How to do it...

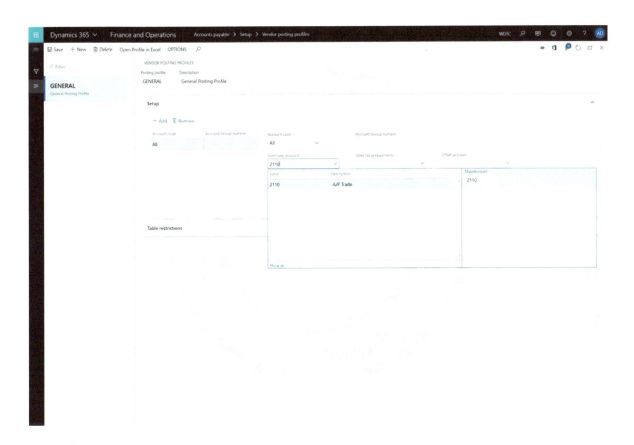

Step 6: Choose the Summary Account

Now we will specify that the summary account for the vendors will be the A/P Trade account.

To do this, we will just need to select the **Summary Account** option from the dropdown list.

For this example, we will want to click on the **Summary Account** dropdown list and pick **2110 (A/P Trade)**.

www.dynamicscompanions.com
Dynamics Companions

- 33 -

www.blindsquirrelpublishing.com
© 2019 Blind Squirrel Publishing, LLC , All Rights Reserved

BLIND SQUIRREL
PUBLISHING

Creating a General Vendor Posting Profile

How to do it...

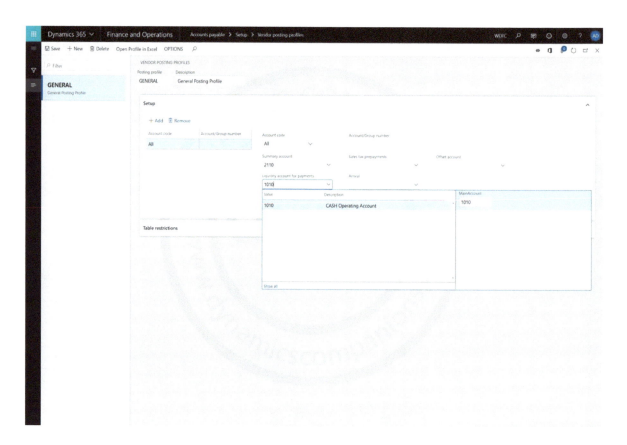

Step 7: Select the Liquidity account for payments

And then we will want to specify that the payment will be posted to the cash account in the ledger.

To do this we will just need to pick the **Liquidity account for payments** option from the dropdown list.

This time, we will want to click on the **Liquidity account for payments** dropdown list and pick **1010 (CASH Operating Account)**.

Creating a General Vendor Posting Profile

How to do it...

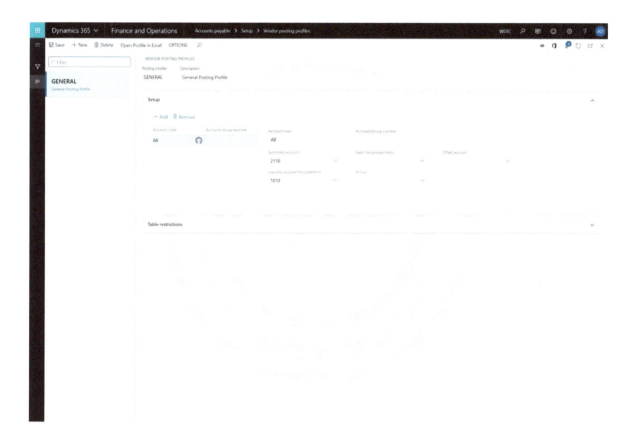

Step 8: Click on the Save button

After we have done that we can save the posting profile and we are done.

To do this just click on the **Save** button.

Review

That wasn't too hard. Now we have a posting profile that we can use in the next step.

Configuring the default Posting Profile

Once we have set up our Vendor posting profiles, we can set them up as the default profile for the company.

Topics Covered

- Opening the Accounts payable parameters form

- Updating the Receiving Posting profiles

Opening the Accounts payable parameters form

To do this we will want to find the **Accounts payable parameters** maintenance form.

How to do it...

Step 1: Open the Accounts payable parameters form through the menu search

We can find the **Accounts payable parameters** form through the menu search feature.

We can do this by clicking on the search icon in the header of the form (or by pressing **ALT+G**)

and then type in **accounts pa p** into the search box. Then you will be able to select the **Accounts payable parameters** form from the dropdown list.

This will open up the Accounts payable parameters form where we can tweak some of the configurations and rules for the module.

Opening the Accounts payable parameters form

How to do it...

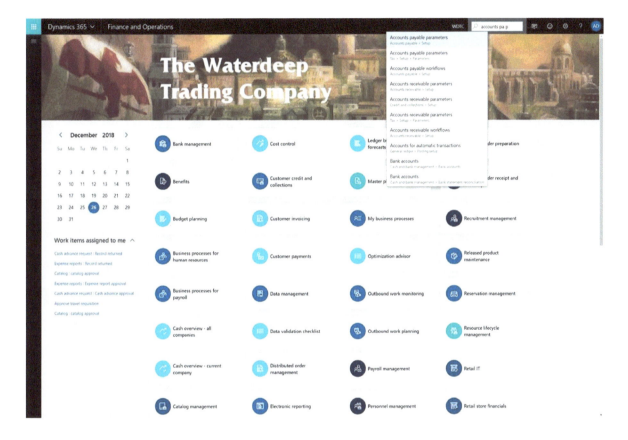

Step 1: Open the Accounts payable parameters form through the menu search

We can find the **Accounts payable parameters** form through the menu search feature.

We can do this by clicking on the search icon in the header of the form (or by pressing **ALT+G**) and then type in **accounts pa p** into the search box. Then you will be able to select the **Accounts payable parameters** form from the dropdown list.

dync
www.dynamicscompanions.com
Dynamics Companions

- 39 -

www.blindsquirrelpublishing.com
© 2019 Blind Squirrel Publishing, LLC, All Rights Reserved

BLIND SQUIRREL
PUBLISHING

Opening the Accounts payable parameters form

How to do it...

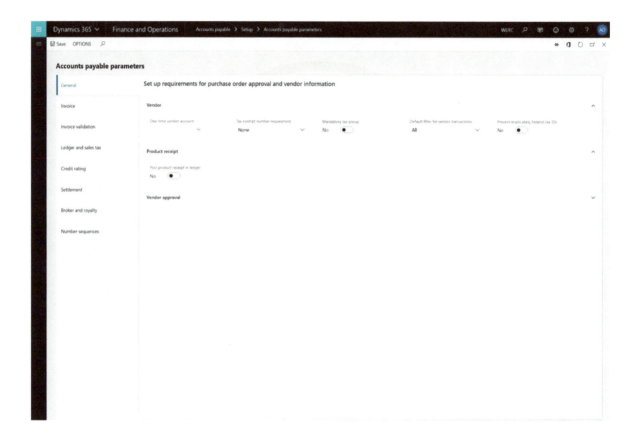

Step 1: Open the Accounts payable parameters form through the menu search

This will open up the Accounts payable parameters form where we can tweak some of the configurations and rules for the module.

dync
www.dynamicscompanions.com
Dynamics Companions

- 40 -

www.blindsquirrelpublishing.com
© 2019 Blind Squirrel Publishing, LLC, All Rights Reserved

BLIND SQUIRREL
PUBLISHING

Updating the Receiving Posting profiles

Now that we are in the Accounts payable parameters form we will make a few changes to configure the default vendor posting profiles.

How to do it...

Step 1: Change the Post product receipts in ledger

We will start off by telling the system that we want to post the receipt of products at the time that the product is received – as opposed to posting it when the invoice is generated.

To do this just toggle the **Post product receipts in ledger** option.

This time, we will want to click on the **Post product receipts in ledger** toggle switch and change it to the **Yes** value.

Step 2: Expand Ledger and sales tax tab

Now we want to configure a default posting profile, and we will do that within the **Ledger and sales tax** tab of the parameters form.

To do this just expand the **Ledger and sales tax** tab.

Step 3: Choose the Posting profile

From here we will be able to select the General posting profile that we set up in the previous step as our default posting profile.

To do this just select the **Posting profile** value from the dropdown list.

This time, we will want to click on the **Posting profile** dropdown list and select **GENERAL**.

Step 4: Click on the Save button

After we have done that we can save the changes and we are done.

To do this, all we need to do is click on the **Save** button.

www.dynamicscompanions.com
Dynamics Companions

- 41 -

www.blindsquirrelpublishing.com
© 2019 Blind Squirrel Publishing, LLC , All Rights Reserved

BLIND SQUIRREL
PUBLISHING

Updating the Receiving Posting profiles

How to do it...

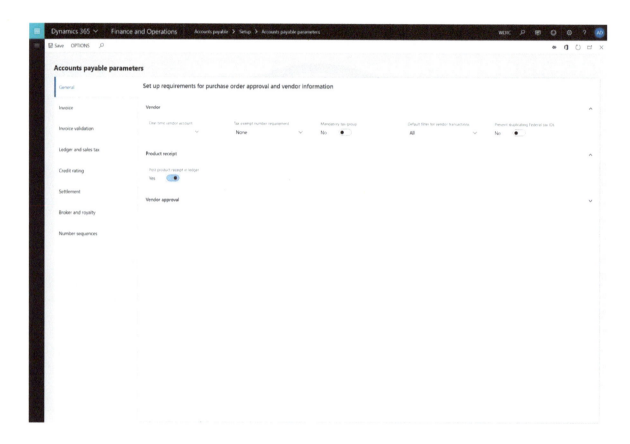

Step 1: Change the Post product receipts in ledger

We will start off by telling the system that we want to post the receipt of products at the time that the product is received – as opposed to posting it when the invoice is generated.

To do this just toggle the **Post product receipts in ledger** option.

This time, we will want to click on the **Post product receipts in ledger** toggle switch and change it to the **Yes** value.

dync
dynamics companions

www.dynamicscompanions.com
Dynamics Companions

- 42 -

www.blindsquirrelpublishing.com
© 2019 Blind Squirrel Publishing, LLC , All Rights Reserved

BLIND SQUIRREL
PUBLISHING

Updating the Receiving Posting profiles

How to do it...

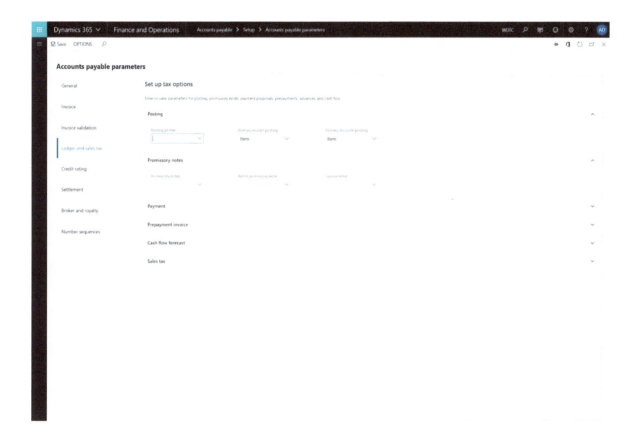

Step 2: Expand Ledger and sales tax tab

Now we want to configure a default posting profile, and we will do that within the **Ledger and sales tax** tab of the parameters form.

To do this just expand the **Ledger and sales tax** tab.

dync
www.dynamicscompanions.com
Dynamics Companions

- 43 -

www.blindsquirrelpublishing.com
© 2019 Blind Squirrel Publishing, LLC , All Rights Reserved

BLIND SQUIRREL
PUBLISHING

Updating the Receiving Posting profiles

How to do it...

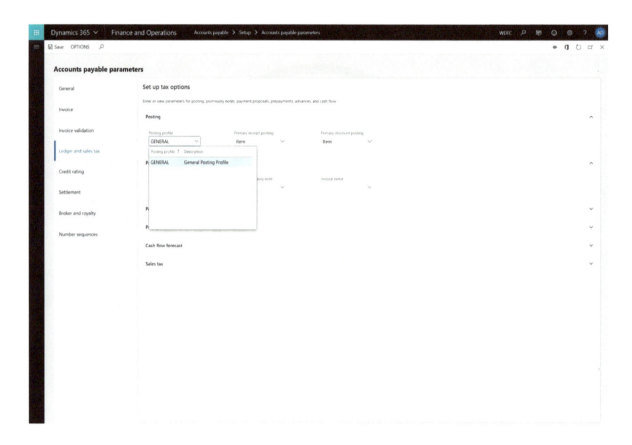

Step 3: Choose the Posting profile

From here we will be able to select the General posting profile that we set up in the previous step as our default posting profile.

To do this just select the **Posting profile** value from the dropdown list.

This time, we will want to click on the **Posting profile** dropdown list and select **GENERAL**.

www.dynamicscompanions.com
Dynamics Companions

- 44 -

www.blindsquirrelpublishing.com
© 2019 Blind Squirrel Publishing, LLC , All Rights Reserved

BLIND SQUIRREL
PUBLISHING

Updating the Receiving Posting profiles

How to do it...

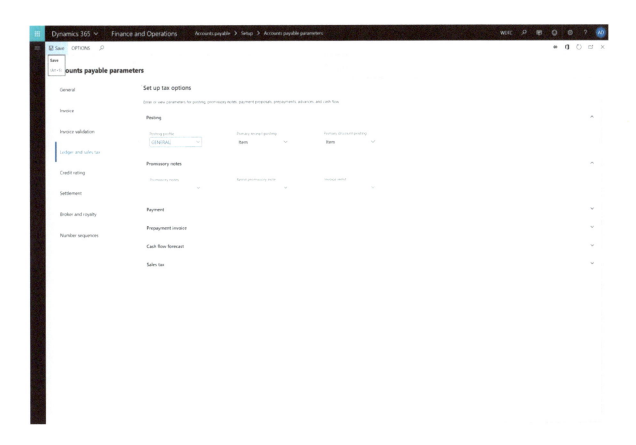

Step 4: Click on the Save button

After we have done that we can save the changes and we are done.

To do this, all we need to do is click on the **Save** button.

www.dynamicscompanions.com
Dynamics Companions

- 45 -

www.blindsquirrelpublishing.com
© 2019 Blind Squirrel Publishing, LLC , All Rights Reserved

BLIND SQUIRREL
PUBLISHING

Review

That wasn't hard. Now we have linked out posting profile with the default parameters.

Summary

Congratulations. We have now configured all of the ledger defaults that we will need in order to track all of our purchases within the ledger.

Creating Vendor Profiles

Now we will want to set up the vendors that we will be using within the system, and associating them with different vendor groups.

Topics Covered

- Creating a New Vendor Groups

- Creating a New Vendor

Creating a New Vendor Groups

Before we set up the vendors though we will first create some vendor groups that we will use to classify the vendors and also set some defaults regarding how the vendor is managed within the system.

Topics Covered

- Opening the Vendor Groups maintenance form

- Creating new Vendor Groups

Opening the Vendor Groups maintenance form

To do this we will want to find the **Vendor groups** maintenance form.

How to do it...

Step 1: Open the Vendor groups form through the menu search

We can find the **Vendor groups** form through the menu search feature.

We can do this by clicking on the search icon in the header of the form (or by pressing **ALT+G**)

and then type in **vendor gr** into the search box. Then you will be able to select the **Vendor groups** form from the dropdown list.

This will open up the Vendor groups maintenance form where we will be able to set up the different vendor classifications.

Opening the Vendor Groups maintenance form

How to do it...

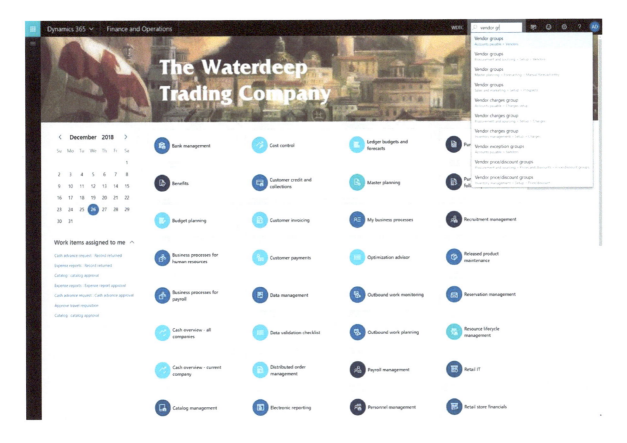

Step 1: Open the Vendor groups form through the menu search

We can find the **Vendor groups** form through the menu search feature.

We can do this by clicking on the search icon in the header of the form (or by pressing **ALT+G**) and then type in **vendor gr** into the search box. Then you will be able to select the **Vendor groups** form from the dropdown list.

dync
www.dynamicscompanions.com
Dynamics Companions

- 51 -

www.blindsquirrelpublishing.com
© 2019 Blind Squirrel Publishing, LLC , All Rights Reserved

BLIND SQUIRREL
PUBLISHING

Opening the Vendor Groups maintenance form

How to do it...

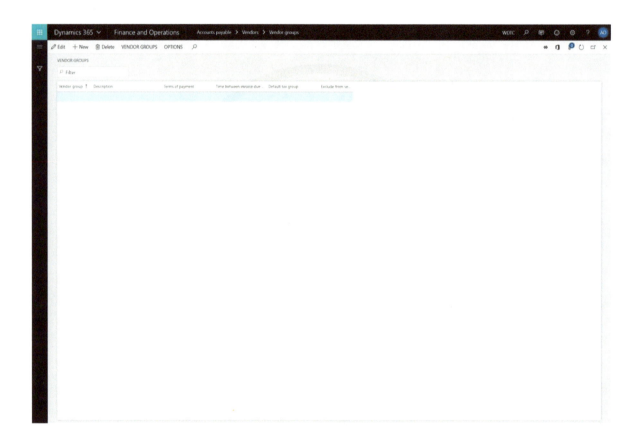

Step 1: Open the Vendor groups form through the menu search

This will open up the Vendor groups maintenance form where we will be able to set up the different vendor classifications.

dync
www.dynamicscompanions.com
Dynamics Companions

- 52 -

www.blindsquirrelpublishing.com
© 2019 Blind Squirrel Publishing, LLC, All Rights Reserved

BLIND SQUIRREL
PUBLISHING

Creating new Vendor Groups

Let's add some vendor groups to the system next.

How to do it...

Step 1: Click on the New button

All we need to do is create a new Vendor group records. We will start by adding a vendor group for our general trading merchants.

To do this just click on the **New** button.

Step 2: Update the Vendor group

Now we will give our new vendor group a code to reference it.

To do this just update the **Vendor group** value.

For this example, we will want to set the **Vendor group** to **MERCANTILE**.

Step 3: Update the Description

And we will add a description to the vendor group to add a little more color to the group.

To do this, we will just need to update the **Description** value.

For this example, we will want to set the **Description** to **Mercantile Guilds**.

Step 4: Click on the New button

Next, we will create a new vendor group for our governmental suppliers to segregate them out from the common vendors.

To do this just click on the **New** button.

Step 5: Update the Vendor group

We will want to give the vendor groups a unique code to reference it by.

To do this just change the **Vendor group** value.

This time, we will want to set the **Vendor group** to **GOVERNMENT**.

Step 6: Update the Description

And then we will associate a description with the code.

To do this just change the **Description** value.

For this example, we will want to set the **Description** to **Government**.

Step 7: Click on the New button

Let's continue and add a vendor group for all of the mages and mystics that we may be purchasing products and services from.

To do this, all we need to do is click on the **New** button.

Step 8: Update the Vendor group

We will give the vendor group an appropriate code to reference it by.

To do this just update the **Vendor group** value.

www.dynamicscompanions.com
Dynamics Companions

- 53 -

www.blindsquirrelpublishing.com
© 2019 Blind Squirrel Publishing, LLC , All Rights Reserved

BLIND SQUIRREL
PUBLISHING

This time, we will want to set the **Vendor group** to **ARCANE**.

Step 9: Update the Description

And then we will give the vendor group a description.

To do this just update the **Description** value.

For this example, we will want to set the **Description** to **Arcane Guilds**.

Step 10: Click on the New button

Continuing on we will want to set up a vendor group for general laborers that we may purchase services from.

To do this just click on the **New** button.

Step 11: Update the Vendor group and update the Description

And we will give the vendor group a code and a description.

To do this, we will just need to change the **Vendor group** value and change the **Description** value.

This time, we will want to set the **Vendor group** to **LABOR** and set the **Description** to **Labor Guilds**.

Step 12: Click on the New button

Just in case we need to purchase healing services or supplies from clerics, we will add a vendor group for them as well.

To do this just click on the **New** button.

Step 13: Update the Vendor group

We will give this new vendor group a code to reference it by.

To do this just update the **Vendor group** value.

For this example, we will want to set the **Vendor group** to **CLERICAL**.

Step 14: Update the Description

And then we will associate a description for the clerical vendors as well.

To do this, we will just need to change the **Description** value.

For this example, we will want to set the **Description** to **Clerical Guilds**.

Step 15: Click on the New button

Finally, we will create a vendor group to group all of the light-fingered vendors we may need to work with every now and then.

To do this just click on the **New** button.

Step 16: Update the Vendor group

We will give our last vendor group a code to reference it by.

To do this just update the **Vendor group** value.

For this example, we will want to set the **Vendor group** to **THIEVES**.

Step 17: Update the Description

And then we will add a description to accompany the code.

To do this just change the **Description** value.

For this example, we will want to set the **Description** to **Thieves Guilds**.

After we have done that we are all set up.

Creating new Vendor Groups

How to do it...

Step 1: Click on the New button

All we need to do is create a new Vendor group records. We will start by adding a vendor group for our general trading merchants.

To do this just click on the **New** button.

www.dynamicscompanions.com
Dynamics Companions

- 55 -

www.blindsquirrelpublishing.com
© 2019 Blind Squirrel Publishing, LLC , All Rights Reserved

BLIND SQUIRREL
PUBLISHING

Creating new Vendor Groups

How to do it...

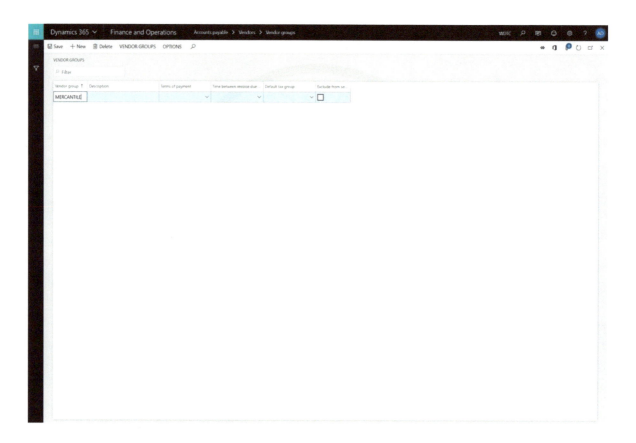

Step 2: Update the Vendor group

Now we will give our new vendor group a code to reference it.

To do this just update the **Vendor group** value.

For this example, we will want to set the **Vendor group** to **MERCANTILE**.

Creating new Vendor Groups

How to do it...

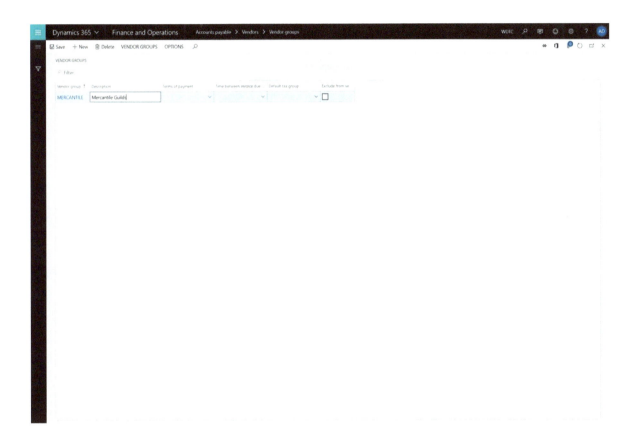

Step 3: Update the Description

And we will add a description to the vendor group to add a little more color to the group.

To do this, we will just need to update the **Description** value.

For this example, we will want to set the **Description** to **Mercantile Guilds**.

dync
dynamics companions

www.dynamicscompanions.com
Dynamics Companions

- 57 -

www.blindsquirrelpublishing.com
© 2019 Blind Squirrel Publishing, LLC , All Rights Reserved

BLIND SQUIRREL
PUBLISHING

Creating new Vendor Groups

How to do it...

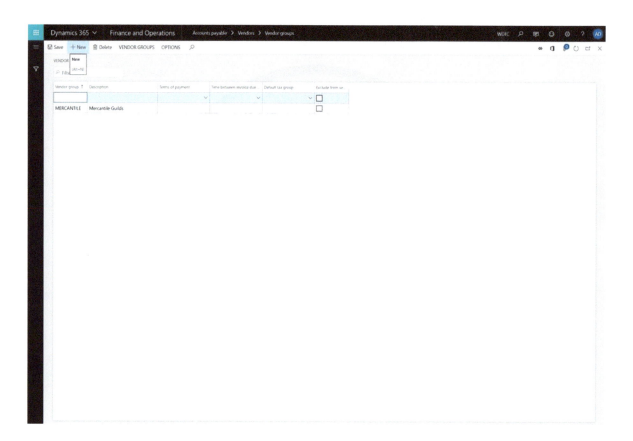

Step 4: Click on the New button

Next, we will create a new vendor group for our governmental suppliers to segregate them out from the common vendors.

To do this just click on the **New** button.

Creating new Vendor Groups

How to do it...

Step 5: Update the Vendor group

We will want to give the vendor groups a unique code to reference it by.

To do this just change the **Vendor group** value.

This time, we will want to set the **Vendor group** to **GOVERNMENT**.

Creating new Vendor Groups

How to do it...

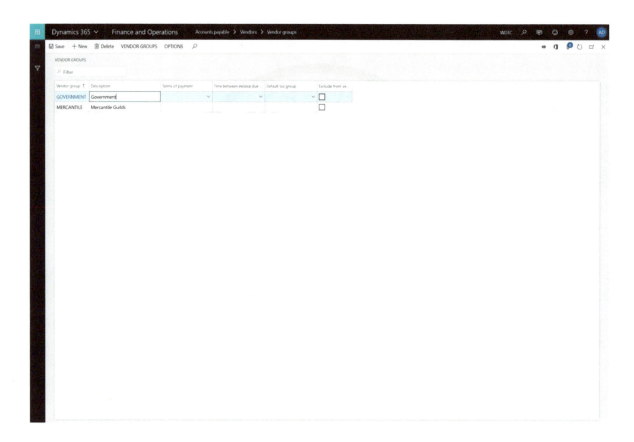

Step 6: Update the Description

And then we will associate a description with the code.

To do this just change the **Description** value.

For this example, we will want to set the **Description** to **Government**.

dync
dynamics companions
www.dynamicscompanions.com
Dynamics Companions

- 60 -

www.blindsquirrelpublishing.com
© 2019 Blind Squirrel Publishing, LLC , All Rights Reserved

BLIND SQUIRREL
PUBLISHING

Creating new Vendor Groups

How to do it...

Step 7: Click on the New button

Let's continue and add a vendor group for all of the mages and mystics that we may be purchasing products and services from.

To do this, all we need to do is click on the **New** button.

Creating new Vendor Groups

How to do it...

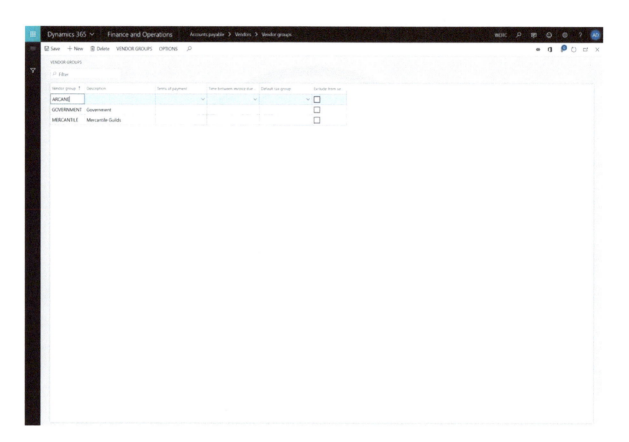

Step 8: Update the Vendor group

We will give the vendor group an appropriate code to reference it by.

To do this just update the **Vendor group** value.

This time, we will want to set the **Vendor group** to **ARCANE**.

dync
dynamics companions

www.dynamicscompanions.com
Dynamics Companions

- 62 -

www.blindsquirrelpublishing.com
© 2019 Blind Squirrel Publishing, LLC , All Rights Reserved

BLIND SQUIRREL
PUBLISHING

Creating new Vendor Groups

How to do it...

Step 9: Update the Description

And then we will give the vendor group a description.

To do this just update the **Description** value.

For this example, we will want to set the **Description** to **Arcane Guilds**.

dync
dynamics companions

www.dynamicscompanions.com
Dynamics Companions

- 63 -

www.blindsquirrelpublishing.com
© 2019 Blind Squirrel Publishing, LLC, All Rights Reserved

BLIND SQUIRREL
PUBLISHING

Creating new Vendor Groups

How to do it...

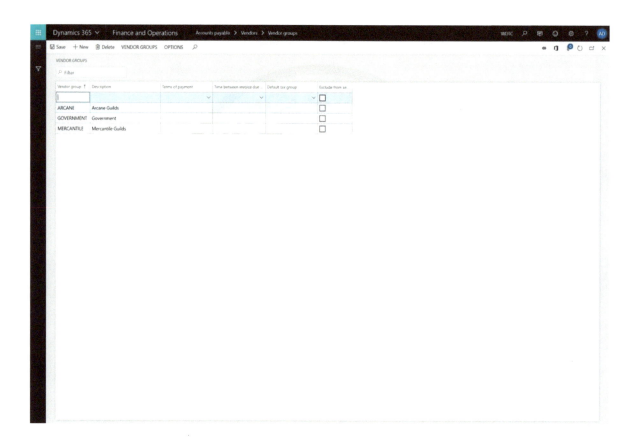

Step 10: Click on the New button

Continuing on we will want to set up a vendor group for general laborers that we may purchase services from.

To do this just click on the **New** button.

Creating new Vendor Groups

How to do it...

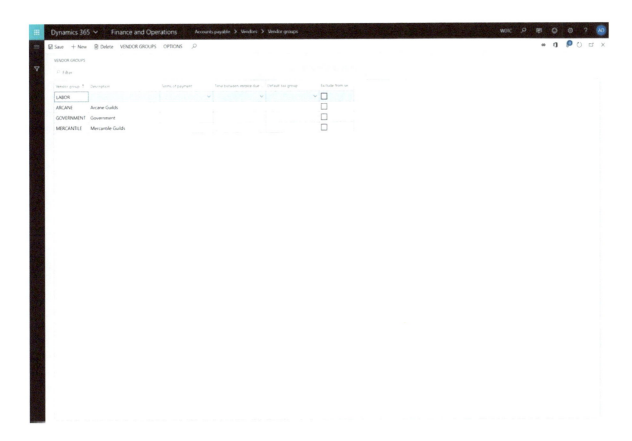

Step 11: Update the Vendor group and update the Description

And we will give the vendor group a code and a description.

To do this, we will just need to change the **Vendor group** value and change the **Description** value.

This time, we will want to set the **Vendor group** to **LABOR** and set the **Description** to **Labor Guilds**.

dync
dynamics companion
www.dynamicscompanions.com
Dynamics Companions

- 65 -

www.blindsquirrelpublishing.com
© 2019 Blind Squirrel Publishing, LLC , All Rights Reserved

BLIND SQUIRREL
PUBLISHING

Creating new Vendor Groups

How to do it...

Step 12: Click on the New button

Just in case we need to purchase healing services or supplies from clerics, we will add a vendor group for them as well.

To do this just click on the **New** button.

dync
dynamics companions
www.dynamicscompanions.com
Dynamics Companions

- 66 -

www.blindsquirrelpublishing.com
© 2019 Blind Squirrel Publishing, LLC , All Rights Reserved

BLIND SQUIRREL
PUBLISHING

Creating new Vendor Groups

How to do it...

Step 13: Update the Vendor group

We will give this new vendor group a code to reference it by.

To do this just update the **Vendor group** value.

For this example, we will want to set the **Vendor group** to **CLERICAL**.

dync
www.dynamicscompanions.com
Dynamics Companions

- 67 -

www.blindsquirrelpublishing.com
© 2019 Blind Squirrel Publishing, LLC , All Rights Reserved

BLIND SQUIRREL
PUBLISHING

Creating new Vendor Groups

How to do it...

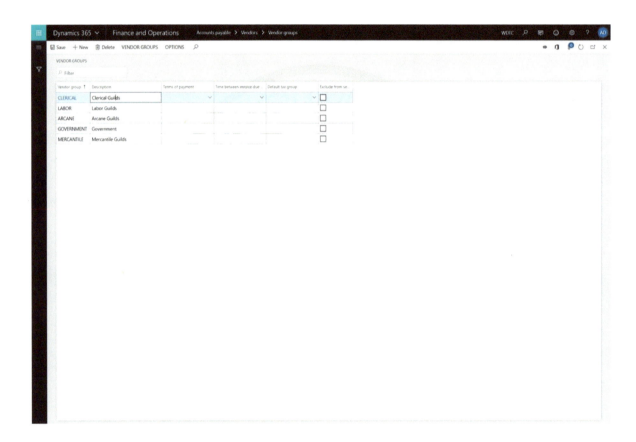

Step 14: Update the Description

And then we will associate a description for the clerical vendors as well.

To do this, we will just need to change the **Description** value.

For this example, we will want to set the **Description** to **Clerical Guilds**.

dync
www.dynamicscompanions.com
Dynamics Companions

- 68 -

www.blindsquirrelpublishing.com
© 2019 Blind Squirrel Publishing, LLC , All Rights Reserved

BLIND SQUIRREL
PUBLISHING

Creating new Vendor Groups

How to do it...

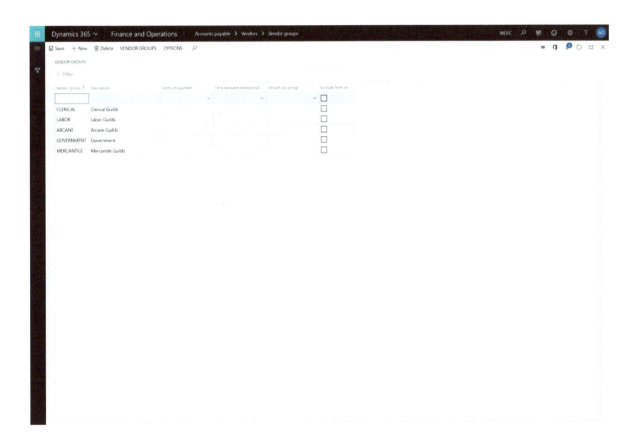

Step 15: Click on the New button

Finally, we will create a vendor group to group all of the light-fingered vendors we may need to work with every now and then.

To do this just click on the **New** button.

Creating new Vendor Groups

How to do it...

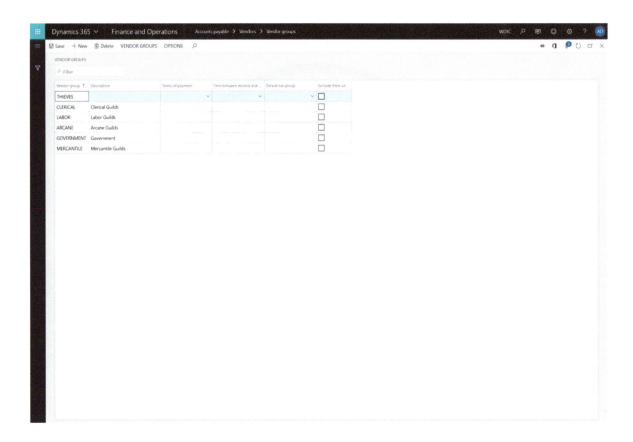

Step 16: Update the Vendor group

We will give our last vendor group a code to reference it by.

To do this just update the **Vendor group** value.

For this example, we will want to set the **Vendor group** to **THIEVES**.

dync
dynamics companions

www.dynamicscompanions.com
Dynamics Companions

- 70 -

www.blindsquirrelpublishing.com
© 2019 Blind Squirrel Publishing, LLC , All Rights Reserved

BLIND SQUIRREL
PUBLISHING

Creating new Vendor Groups

How to do it...

Step 17: Update the Description

And then we will add a description to accompany the code.

To do this just change the **Description** value.

For this example, we will want to set the **Description** to **Thieves Guilds**.

Creating new Vendor Groups

How to do it...

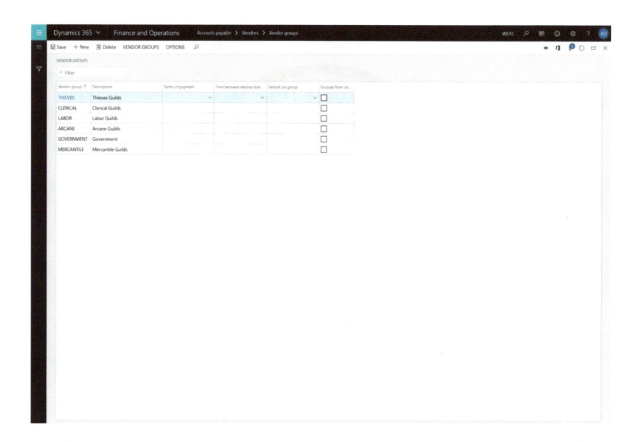

Step 17: Update the Description

After we have done that we are all set up.

dync
dynamics companions
www.dynamicscompanions.com
Dynamics Companions

- 72 -

www.blindsquirrelpublishing.com
© 2019 Blind Squirrel Publishing, LLC, All Rights Reserved

BLIND SQUIRREL
PUBLISHING

Review

Now that we have our vendor groups configured, we can classify our vendors as we set them up. This is great for reporting and grouping of our purchases by area and by the guild.

www.dynamicscompanions.com
Dynamics Companions

- 73 -

www.blindsquirrelpublishing.com
© 2019 Blind Squirrel Publishing, LLC , All Rights Reserved

BLIND SQUIRREL
PUBLISHING

Creating a New Vendor

Now that we have our vendor groups set up we can go ahead and start setting up our vendors that we will be working with and purchasing products and services from.

Topics Covered

- Opening the Vendor maintenance form

- Adding a new Vendor

- Updating the Vendor Purchasing Defaults

Opening the Vendor maintenance form

In order to create our vendors, we will want to track form the **All Vendors** maintenance form.

How to do it...

Step 1: Open the All vendors form through the menu search

We can find the **All vendors** form through the menu search feature.

We can do this by clicking on the search icon in the header of the form (or by pressing **ALT+G**)

and then type in **all vend** into the search box. Then you will be able to select the **All vendors** form from the dropdown list.

This will open up the **Vendors** maintenance form where we will be able to create and manage our vendors.

Opening the Vendor maintenance form

How to do it...

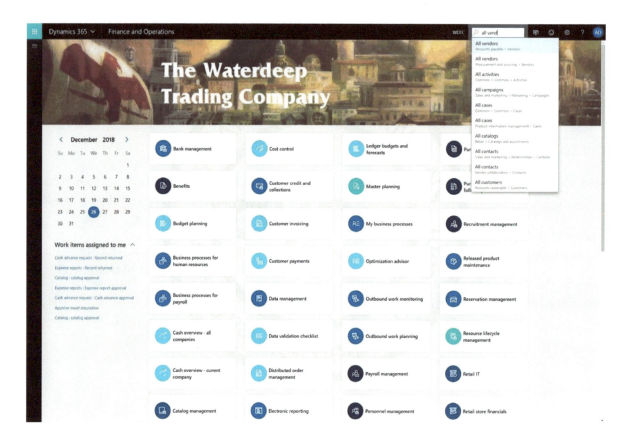

Step 1: Open the All vendors form through the menu search

We can find the **All vendors** form through the menu search feature.

We can do this by clicking on the search icon in the header of the form (or by pressing **ALT+G**) and then type in **all vend** into the search box. Then you will be able to select the **All vendors** form from the dropdown list.

Opening the Vendor maintenance form

How to do it...

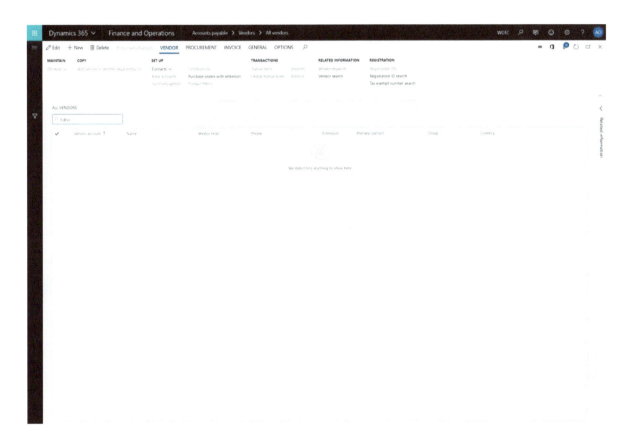

Step 1: Open the All vendors form through the menu search

This will open up the **Vendors** maintenance form where we will be able to create and manage our vendors.

www.dynamicscompanions.com
Dynamics Companions

- 77 -

www.blindsquirrelpublishing.com
© 2019 Blind Squirrel Publishing, LLC, All Rights Reserved

BLIND SQUIRREL
PUBLISHING

Adding a new Vendor

We will start off by creating our very first vendor record in the system.

How to do it...

Step 1: Click on the New button

We will start by creating a new vendor record.

To do this just click on the **New** button.

This will create a new vendor record for us that we can start configuring.

Step 2: Update the Name

The first vendor that we will set up will be the **Waterdeep Leather** vendor, which is the best place for us to buy the finest leather goods including backpacks, which will be great seller within the store.

So we will want first to set the name of the vendor.

To do this just update the **Name** value.

This time, we will want to set the **Name** to **Waterdeep Leather**.

This will automatically populate the **Search name** for us which we will keep the same for now.

Step 3: Choose the Group

Next, we will want to assign the vendor to a group.

To do this just pick the **Group** value from the dropdown list.

For this example, we will want to click on the **Group** dropdown list and pick **MERCANTILE**.

Adding a new Vendor

How to do it...

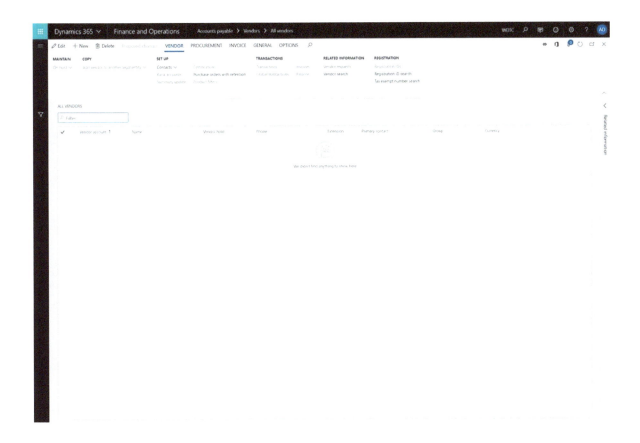

Step 1: Click on the New button

We will start by creating a new vendor record.

To do this just click on the **New** button.

Adding a new Vendor

How to do it...

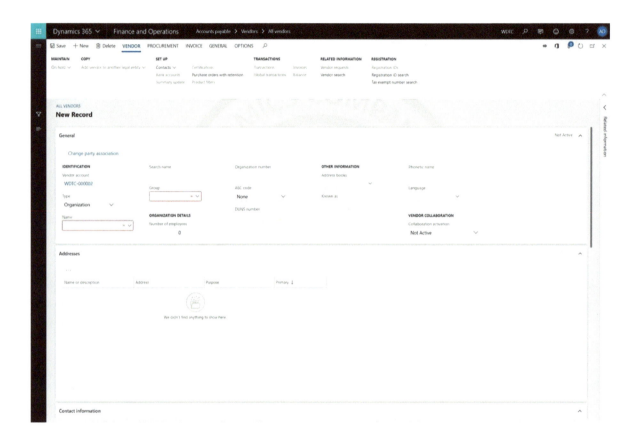

Step 1: Click on the New button

This will create a new vendor record for us that we can start configuring.

Adding a new Vendor

How to do it...

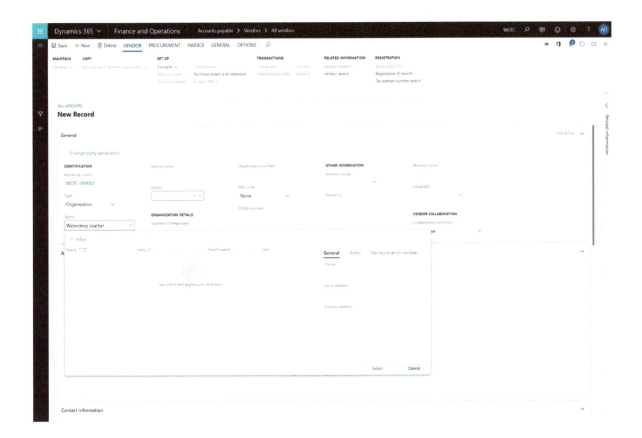

Step 2: Update the Name

The first vendor that we will set up will be the **Waterdeep Leather** vendor, which is the best place for us to buy the finest leather goods including backpacks, which will be great seller within the store.

So we will want first to set the name of the vendor.

To do this just update the **Name** value.

This time, we will want to set the **Name** to **Waterdeep Leather**.

www.dynamicscompanions.com
Dynamics Companions

- 81 -

www.blindsquirrelpublishing.com
© 2019 Blind Squirrel Publishing, LLC , All Rights Reserved

BLIND SQUIRREL
PUBLISHING

Adding a new Vendor

How to do it...

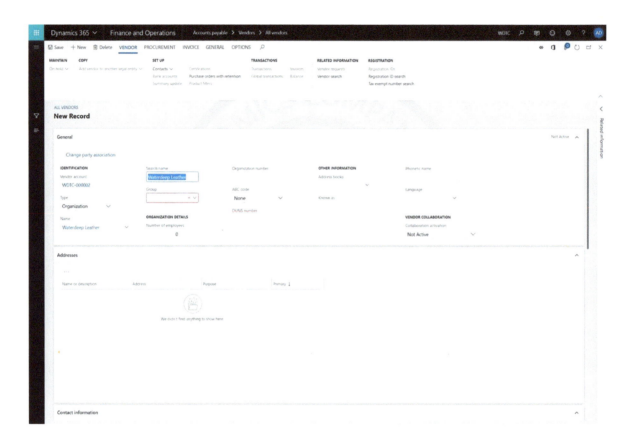

Step 2: Update the Name

This will automatically populate the **Search name** for us which we will keep the same for now.

dync
www.dynamicscompanions.com
Dynamics Companions

- 82 -

www.blindsquirrelpublishing.com
© 2019 Blind Squirrel Publishing, LLC , All Rights Reserved

BLIND SQUIRREL
PUBLISHING

Adding a new Vendor

How to do it...

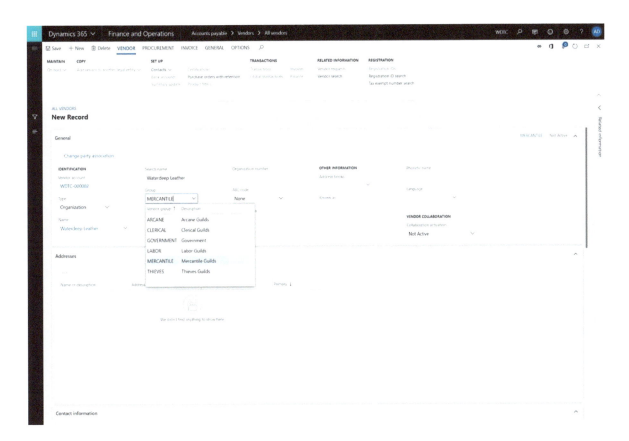

Step 3: Choose the Group

Next, we will want to assign the vendor to a group.

To do this just pick the **Group** value from the dropdown list.

For this example, we will want to click on the **Group** dropdown list and pick **MERCANTILE**.

Updating the Vendor Purchasing Defaults

Before we leave the vendor we will want to add some defaults to the vendor to save us time later on.

How to do it...

Step 1: Expand Purchase order defaults tab

We will need to find the section of the vendor maintenance where all of the purchasing defaults are managed.

To do this, all we need to do is expand the **Purchase order defaults** tab.

Step 2: Select the Site

From here we can default on the site and the location that we will usually be purchased from this vendor.

We will start off by assigning a default site to the vendor.

To do this just select the **Site** value from the dropdown list.

For this example, we will want to click on the **Site** dropdown list and pick **WD**.

Step 3: Select the Warehouse

And then we will specify the **Waterdeep Store** as the default receiving location.

To do this just select the **Warehouse** value from the dropdown list.

For this example, we will want to click on the **Warehouse** dropdown list and select **WDSTORE**.

Step 4: Click on the Save button

After we have done that we can just save the vendor and we are done with the setup.

To do this, all we need to do is click on the **Save** button.

Updating the Vendor Purchasing Defaults

How to do it...

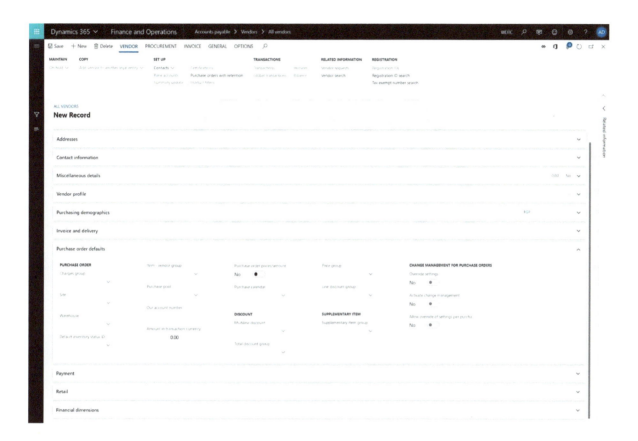

Step 1: Expand Purchase order defaults tab

We will need to find the section of the vendor maintenance where all of the purchasing defaults are managed.

To do this, all we need to do is expand the **Purchase order defaults** tab.

www.dynamicscompanions.com
Dynamics Companions

- 85 -

www.blindsquirrelpublishing.com
© 2019 Blind Squirrel Publishing, LLC , All Rights Reserved

BLIND SQUIRREL
PUBLISHING

Updating the Vendor Purchasing Defaults

How to do it...

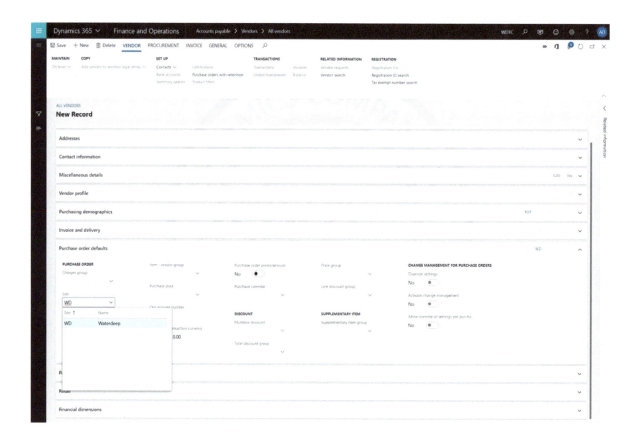

Step 2: Select the Site

From here we can default on the site and the location that we will usually be purchased from this vendor.

We will start off by assigning a default site to the vendor.

To do this just select the **Site** value from the dropdown list.

For this example, we will want to click on the **Site** dropdown list and pick **WD**.

Updating the Vendor Purchasing Defaults

How to do it...

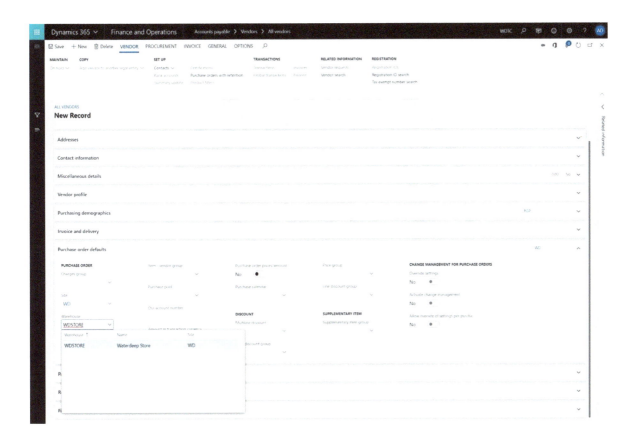

Step 3: Select the Warehouse

And then we will specify the **Waterdeep Store** as the default receiving location.

To do this just select the **Warehouse** value from the dropdown list.

For this example, we will want to click on the **Warehouse** dropdown list and select **WDSTORE**.

dync
www.dynamicscompanions.com
Dynamics Companions

- 87 -

www.blindsquirrelpublishing.com
© 2019 Blind Squirrel Publishing, LLC, All Rights Reserved

BLIND SQUIRREL
PUBLISHING

Updating the Vendor Purchasing Defaults

How to do it...

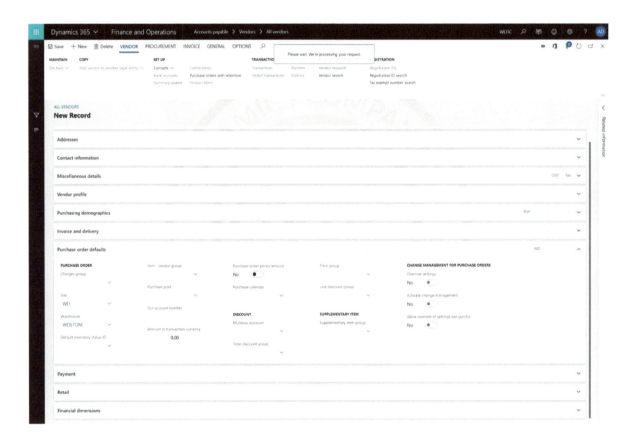

Step 4: Click on the Save button

After we have done that we can just save the vendor and we are done with the setup.

To do this, all we need to do is click on the **Save** button.

dync
dynamics companions

www.dynamicscompanions.com
Dynamics Companions

- 88 -

www.blindsquirrelpublishing.com
© 2019 Blind Squirrel Publishing, LLC , All Rights Reserved

BLIND SQUIRREL
PUBLISHING

Review

How easy was that? Setting up a vendor only requires a couple of data elements to be defined.

www.dynamicscompanions.com
Dynamics Companions

- 89 -

www.blindsquirrelpublishing.com
© 2019 Blind Squirrel Publishing, LLC , All Rights Reserved

BLIND SQUIRREL
PUBLISHING

Summary

Congratulations. We are now well on the way to set up the purchasing system with the new vendors that we added to the system.

Purchasing Products

Now that we have all of the controls configured, and also preferred vendors that we can work with, we can start moving on to the end goal, which is to start buying products and then receiving them into the store.

Topics Covered

- Creating a Purchase Order

- Receiving Purchase Orders Into Inventory

- Viewing the Inventory On Hand

Creating a Purchase Order

So let's do that and start by creating a new purchase order for some backpacks.

Topics Covered

- Opening the Purchase Order Preparation workspace

- Creating a new Purchase Order

- Adding lines to the Purchase order

- Specifying the default receiving location

- Confirming the Purchase Order

Opening the Purchase Order Preparation workspace

We will use the **Purchase order preparation** workspace to track all of our purchases, so let's open that workspace.

How to do it...

Step 1: Open the Purchase order preparation workspace through the menu search

We can find the **Purchase order preparation** workspace through the menu search feature.

We can do this by clicking on the search icon in the header of the form (or by pressing **ALT+G**)

and then type in **purchase order p** into the search box. Then you will be able to select the **Purchase order preparation** workspace from the dropdown list.

This will open up the **Purchase order preparation** workspace for us where we will track all of our purchase orders and also from which we can create new Purchase orders.

www.dynamicscompanions.com
Dynamics Companions

- 93 -

www.blindsquirrelpublishing.com
© 2019 Blind Squirrel Publishing, LLC , All Rights Reserved

BLIND SQUIRREL
PUBLISHING

Opening the Purchase Order Preparation workspace

How to do it...

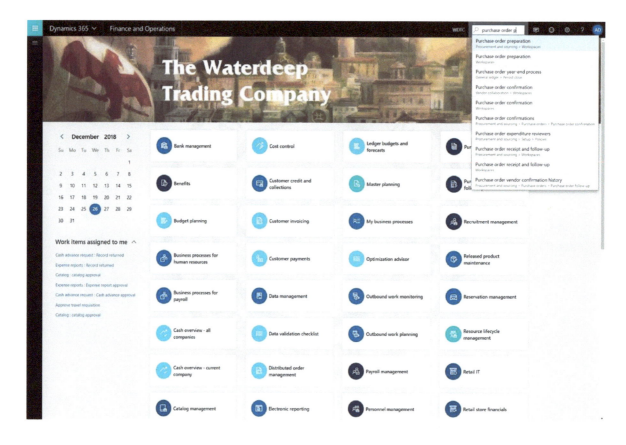

Step 1: Open the Purchase order preparation workspace through the menu search

We can find the **Purchase order preparation** workspace through the menu search feature.

We can do this by clicking on the search icon in the header of the form (or by pressing **ALT+G**) and then type in **purchase order p** into the search box. Then you will be able to select the **Purchase order preparation** workspace from the dropdown list.

www.dynamicscompanions.com
Dynamics Companions

- 94 -

www.blindsquirrelpublishing.com
© 2019 Blind Squirrel Publishing, LLC , All Rights Reserved

BLIND SQUIRREL
PUBLISHING

Opening the Purchase Order Preparation workspace

How to do it...

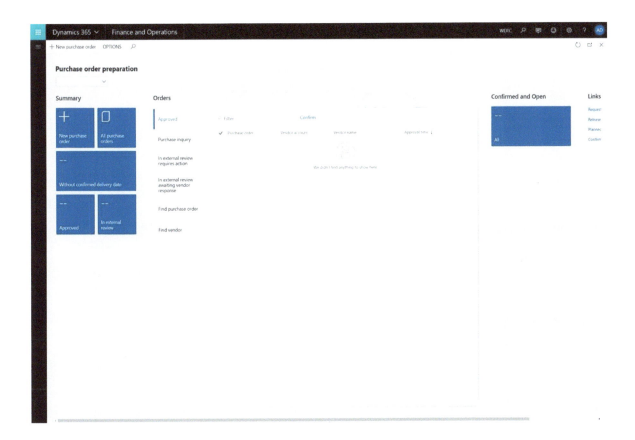

Step 1: Open the Purchase order preparation workspace through the menu search

This will open up the **Purchase order preparation** workspace for us where we will track all of our purchase orders and also from which we can create new Purchase orders.

www.dynamicscompanions.com
Dynamics Companions

- 95 -

www.blindsquirrelpublishing.com
© 2019 Blind Squirrel Publishing, LLC , All Rights Reserved

BLIND SQUIRREL
PUBLISHING

Creating a new Purchase Order

Now that we are in the Purchase order preparation workspace, we will want to create our first purchase order.

How to do it...

Step 1: Click on the New purchase order button

To do this, we will just need to tell the system to create the new purchase order for us.

To do this just click on the **New purchase order** button in the menu bar.

This will open up the **Create purchase order** panel for us where we can start providing the base information for the purchase order.

Step 2: Choose the Vendor account

We will start off by selecting the vendor that we want to create the purchase order for.

To do this we will just need to pick the **Vendor account** option from the dropdown list.

For this example, we will want to click on the **Vendor account** dropdown list and select **WD**.

After we select the vendor account, then a lot of information will automatically default in for us, including the default site and warehouse which we set up on the vendor record when we created it.

Step 3: Select the Purchase type

One item that we will want to change is the type of purchase that we will be creating. By default, it is set to a Journal, which we cannot receive inventory against. We will want to tell the system that this is a purchase order.

To do this we will just need to select the **Purchase type** value from the dropdown list.

For this example, we will want to click on the **Purchase type** dropdown list and pick **Purchase order**.

Step 4: Select the Language

Since we hadn't specified a default language code for the vendor, we will also need to select the default language that we will be sending this purchase order in.

To do this just select the **Language** option from the dropdown list.

This time, we will want to click on the **Language** dropdown list and pick **en-us**.

Step 5: Click on the OK button

After we have done that we can just create the purchase order.

To do this, all we need to do is click on the **OK** button.

www.dynamicscompanions.com
Dynamics Companions

- 96 -

www.blindsquirrelpublishing.com
© 2019 Blind Squirrel Publishing, LLC , All Rights Reserved

BLIND SQUIRREL
PUBLISHING

This will create a new purchase order, and we will be taken to a more detailed view of the purchase order.

Creating a new Purchase Order

How to do it...

Step 1: Click on the New purchase order button

To do this, we will just need to tell the system to create the new purchase order for us.

To do this just click on the **New purchase order** button in the menu bar.

dync
dynamics companions

www.dynamicscompanions.com
Dynamics Companions

- 98 -

www.blindsquirrelpublishing.com
© 2019 Blind Squirrel Publishing, LLC , All Rights Reserved

BLIND SQUIRREL
PUBLISHING

Creating a new Purchase Order

How to do it...

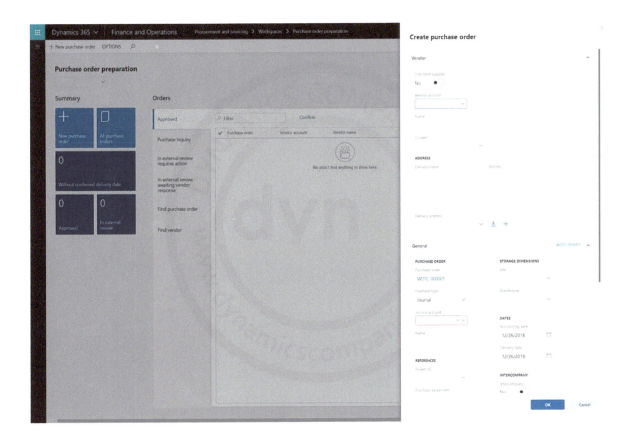

Step 1: Click on the New purchase order button

This will open up the **Create purchase order** panel for us where we can start providing the base information for the purchase order.

dync
www.dynamicscompanions.com
Dynamics Companions

- 99 -

www.blindsquirrelpublishing.com
© 2019 Blind Squirrel Publishing, LLC , All Rights Reserved

BLIND SQUIRREL
PUBLISHING

Creating a new Purchase Order

How to do it...

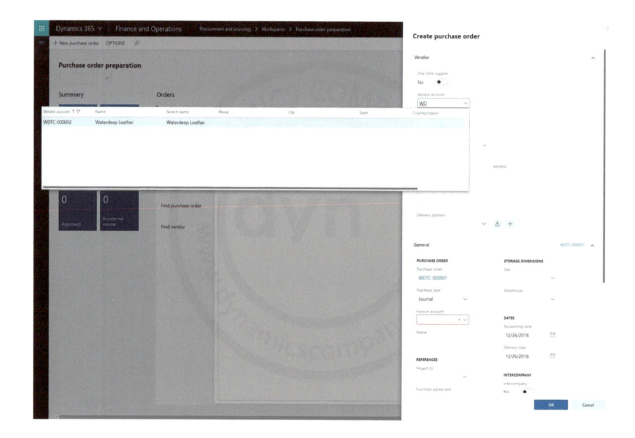

Step 2: Choose the Vendor account

We will start off by selecting the vendor that we want to create the purchase order for.

To do this we will just need to pick the **Vendor account** option from the dropdown list.

For this example, we will want to click on the **Vendor account** dropdown list and select **WD**.

dync
www.dynamicscompanions.com
Dynamics Companions

- 100 -

www.blindsquirrelpublishing.com
© 2019 Blind Squirrel Publishing, LLC , All Rights Reserved

BLIND SQUIRREL
PUBLISHING

Creating a new Purchase Order

How to do it...

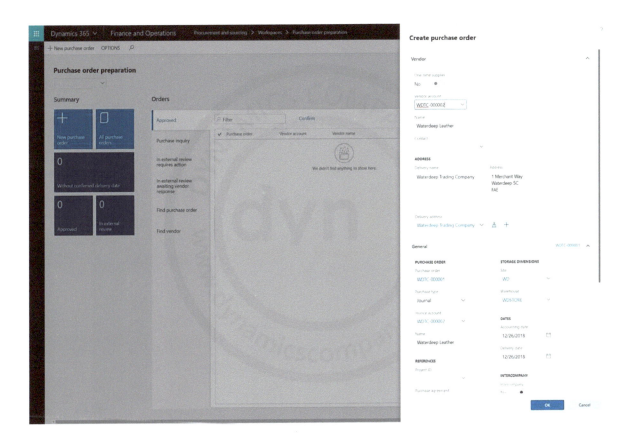

Step 2: Choose the Vendor account

After we select the vendor account, then a lot of information will automatically default in for us, including the default site and warehouse which we set up on the vendor record when we created it.

dync
www.dynamicscompanions.com
Dynamics Companions

- 101 -

www.blindsquirrelpublishing.com
© 2019 Blind Squirrel Publishing, LLC, All Rights Reserved

BLIND SQUIRREL
PUBLISHING

Creating a new Purchase Order

How to do it...

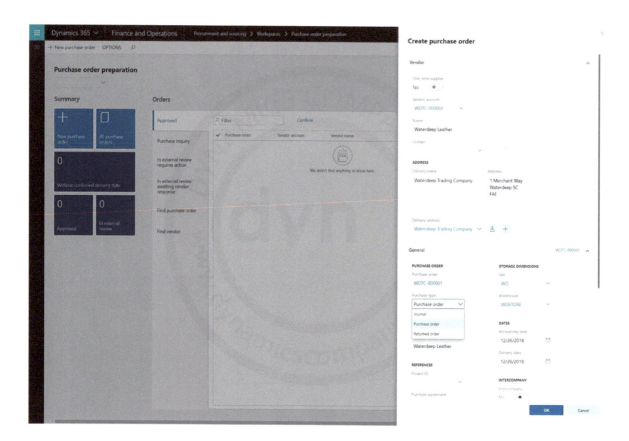

Step 3: Select the Purchase type

One item that we will want to change is the type of purchase that we will be creating. By default, it is set to a Journal, which we cannot receive inventory against. We will want to tell the system that this is a purchase order.

To do this we will just need to select the **Purchase type** value from the dropdown list.

For this example, we will want to click on the **Purchase type** dropdown list and pick **Purchase order**.

dync
dynamics companions

www.dynamicscompanions.com
Dynamics Companions

- 102 -

www.blindsquirrelpublishing.com
© 2019 Blind Squirrel Publishing, LLC, All Rights Reserved

BLIND SQUIRREL
PUBLISHING

Creating a new Purchase Order

How to do it...

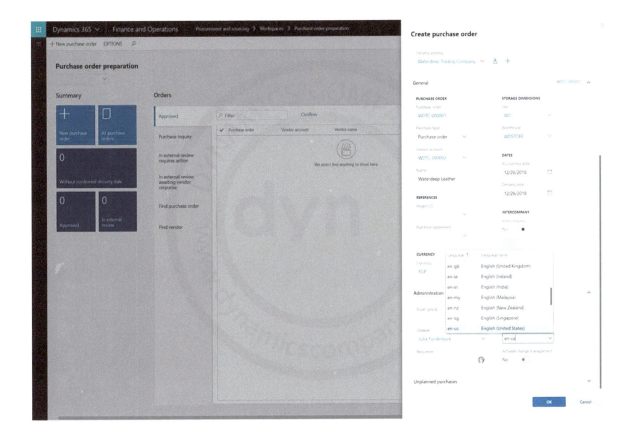

Step 4: Select the Language

Since we hadn't specified a default language code for the vendor, we will also need to select the default language that we will be sending this purchase order in.

To do this just select the **Language** option from the dropdown list.

This time, we will want to click on the **Language** dropdown list and pick **en-us**.

dync

www.dynamicscompanions.com
Dynamics Companions

- 103 -

www.blindsquirrelpublishing.com
© 2019 Blind Squirrel Publishing, LLC , All Rights Reserved

BLIND SQUIRREL
PUBLISHING

Creating a new Purchase Order

How to do it...

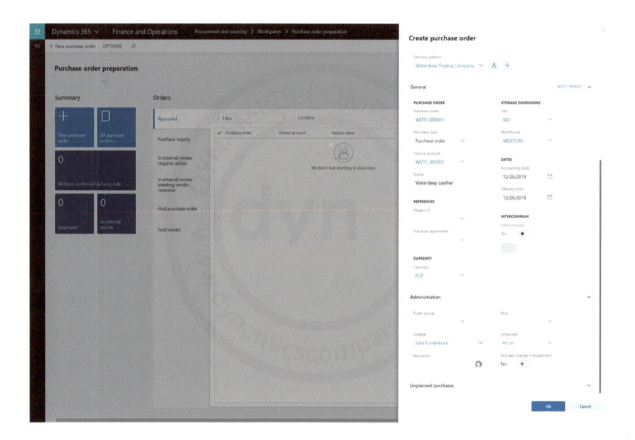

Step 5: Click on the OK button

After we have done that we can just create the purchase order.

To do this, all we need to do is click on the **OK** button.

dync
www.dynamicscompanions.com
Dynamics Companions

- 104 -

www.blindsquirrelpublishing.com
© 2019 Blind Squirrel Publishing, LLC , All Rights Reserved

BLIND SQUIRREL
PUBLISHING

Creating a new Purchase Order

How to do it...

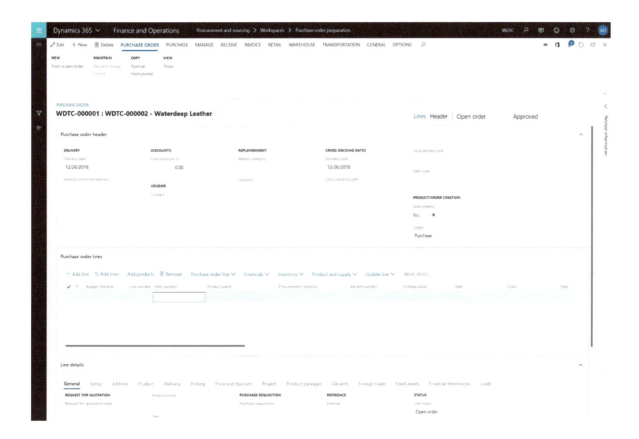

Step 5: Click on the OK button

This will create a new purchase order, and we will be taken to a more detailed view of the purchase order.

www.dynamicscompanions.com
Dynamics Companions

- 105 -

www.blindsquirrelpublishing.com
© 2019 Blind Squirrel Publishing, LLC , All Rights Reserved

BLIND SQUIRREL
PUBLISHING

Adding lines to the Purchase order

Now that we have the header of the purchase order created we will want to start specifying what we want to order from the vendor.

How to do it...

Step 1: Collapse Purchase order header tab

We don't really care about the header information on the purchase order right now, so to get more space on the form to work with we can hide that information away.

To do this, all we need to do is collapse the **Purchase order header** tab.

Step 2: Click on the Edit button

Nest we will want to add some lines to the purchase order, and we will want to switch to edit mode.

To do this, all we need to do is click on the **Edit** button.

Step 3: Choose the Item number

This will allow us to select the item that we want to purchase from the **Waterdeep Leather** company.

To do this just select the **Item number** value from the dropdown list.

For this example, we will want to click on the **Item number** dropdown list and select **BACKPACK**.

Once we have selected the product, the description will default in and any pricing that we may have configured for the product as well.

Step 4: Update the Quantity

We can move on and specify the number of backpacks that we want to purchase.

To do this, we will just need to change the **Quantity** value.

For this example, we will want to set the **Quantity** to **10**.

Step 5: Update the Unit price

And also we can specify the unit price that we have negotiated with the vendor.

To do this just change the **Unit price** value.

This time, we will want to set the **Unit price** to **1**.

Step 6: Click on the Save button

After we have done that we can save the purchase order.

To do this just click on the **Save** button.

Adding lines to the Purchase order

How to do it...

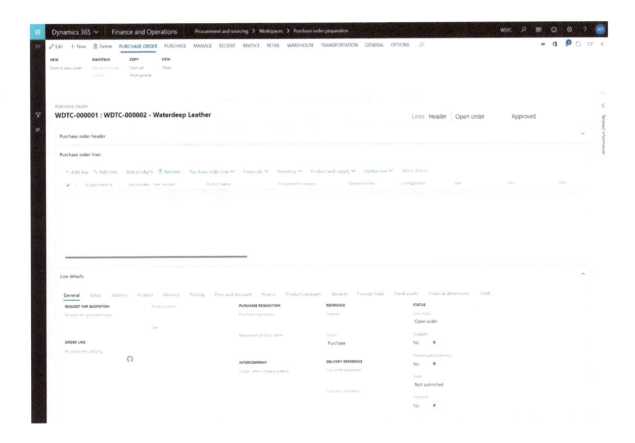

Step 1: Collapse Purchase order header tab

We don't really care about the header information on the purchase order right now, so to get more space on the form to work with we can hide that information away.

To do this, all we need to do is collapse the **Purchase order header** tab.

Adding lines to the Purchase order

How to do it...

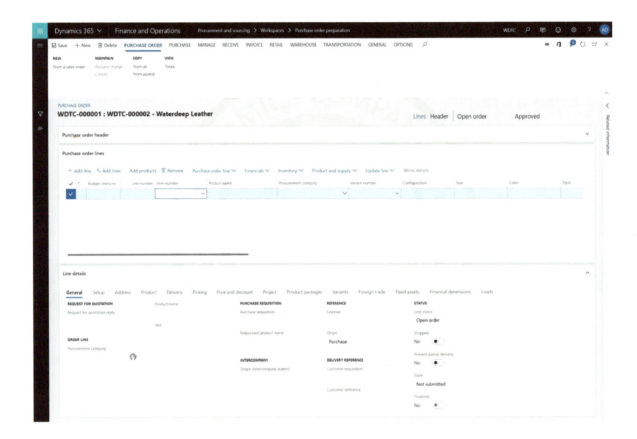

Step 2: Click on the Edit button

Nest we will want to add some lines to the purchase order, and we will want to switch to edit mode.

To do this, all we need to do is click on the **Edit** button.

www.dynamicscompanions.com
Dynamics Companions

- 108 -

www.blindsquirrelpublishing.com
© 2019 Blind Squirrel Publishing, LLC , All Rights Reserved

BLIND SQUIRREL
PUBLISHING

Adding lines to the Purchase order

How to do it...

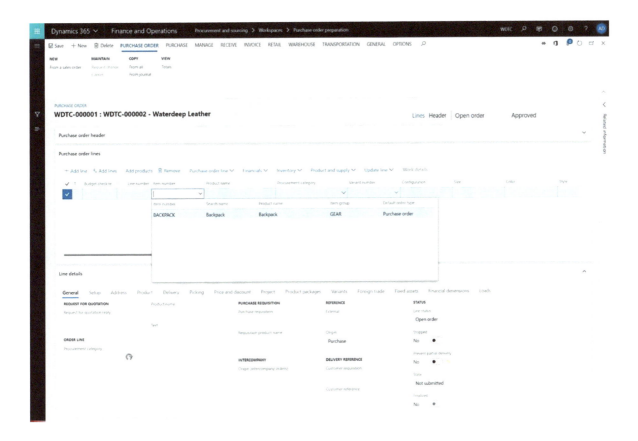

Step 3: Choose the Item number

This will allow us to select the item that we want to purchase from the **Waterdeep Leather** company.

To do this just select the **Item number** value from the dropdown list.

For this example, we will want to click on the **Item number** dropdown list and select **BACKPACK**.

www.dynamicscompanions.com
Dynamics Companions

- 109 -

www.blindsquirrelpublishing.com
© 2019 Blind Squirrel Publishing, LLC , All Rights Reserved

BLIND SQUIRREL
PUBLISHING

Adding lines to the Purchase order

How to do it...

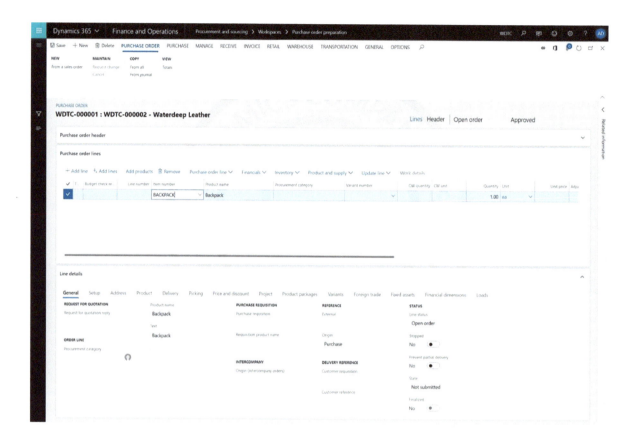

Step 3: Choose the Item number

Once we have selected the product, the description will default in and any pricing that we may have configured for the product as well.

www.dynamicscompanions.com
Dynamics Companions

- 110 -

www.blindsquirrelpublishing.com
© 2019 Blind Squirrel Publishing, LLC , All Rights Reserved

BLIND SQUIRREL
PUBLISHING

Adding lines to the Purchase order

How to do it...

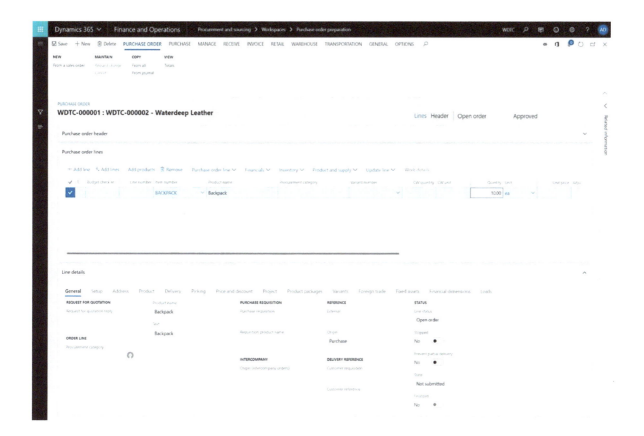

Step 4: Update the Quantity

We can move on and specify the number of backpacks that we want to purchase.

To do this, we will just need to change the **Quantity** value.

For this example, we will want to set the **Quantity** to **10**.

Adding lines to the Purchase order

How to do it...

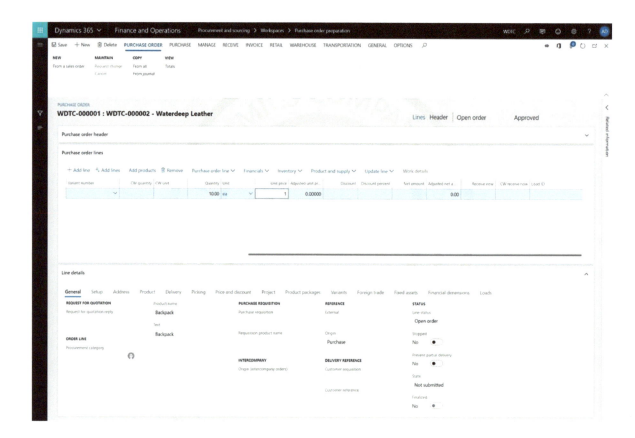

Step 5: Update the Unit price

And also we can specify the unit price that we have negotiated with the vendor.

To do this just change the **Unit price** value.

This time, we will want to set the **Unit price** to **1**.

www.dynamicscompanions.com
Dynamics Companions

- 112 -

www.blindsquirrelpublishing.com
© 2019 Blind Squirrel Publishing, LLC , All Rights Reserved

BLIND SQUIRREL
PUBLISHING

Adding lines to the Purchase order

How to do it...

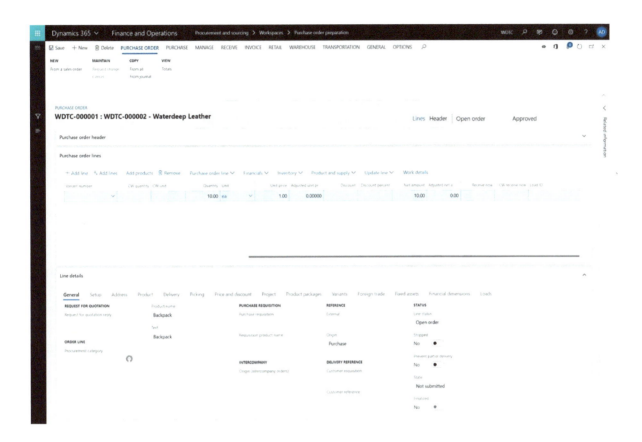

Step 6: Click on the Save button

After we have done that we can save the purchase order.

To do this just click on the **Save** button.

Specifying the default receiving location

Because we have set up the **Waterdeep Trading Company Store** to be managed by location, we will want to make one small change to the purchase order and tell the system where we want to receive the purchase order into and stock it.

How to do it...

Step 1: Select Product tab

The location details for the lines are managed within the Product line details of the purchase order.

To do this just select the **Product** tab.

Step 2: Select the Location

We will want to receive this purchase order directly into the Gear location.

To do this we will just need to select the **Location** option from the dropdown list.

For this example, we will want to click on the **Location** dropdown list and pick **GEAR**.

Step 3: Click on the Save button

After we have done that we are done with the editing of the purchase order.

To do this just click on the **Save** button.

Specifying the default receiving location

How to do it...

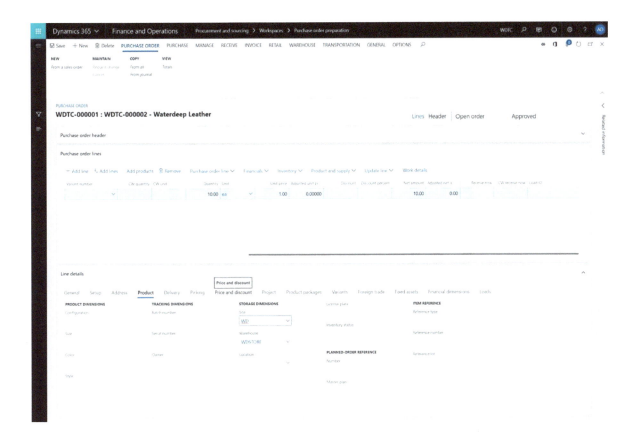

Step 1: Select Product tab

The location details for the lines are managed within the Product line details of the purchase order.

To do this just select the **Product** tab.

www.dynamicscompanions.com
Dynamics Companions

- 115 -

www.blindsquirrelpublishing.com
© 2019 Blind Squirrel Publishing, LLC, All Rights Reserved

BLIND SQUIRREL PUBLISHING

Specifying the default receiving location

How to do it...

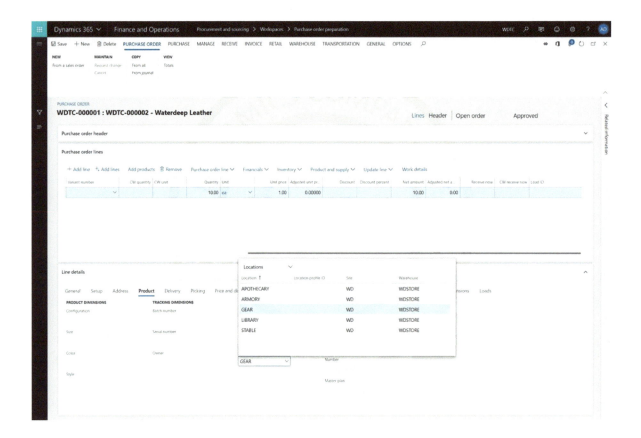

Step 2: Select the Location

We will want to receive this purchase order directly into the Gear location.

To do this we will just need to select the **Location** option from the dropdown list.

For this example, we will want to click on the **Location** dropdown list and pick **GEAR**.

dync
www.dynamicscompanions.com
Dynamics Companions

- 116 -

www.blindsquirrelpublishing.com
© 2019 Blind Squirrel Publishing, LLC , All Rights Reserved

BLIND SQUIRREL
PUBLISHING

Specifying the default receiving location

How to do it...

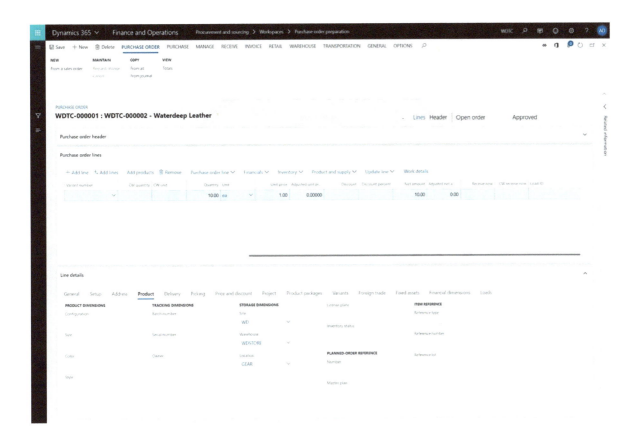

Step 3: Click on the Save button

After we have done that we are done with the editing of the purchase order.

To do this just click on the **Save** button.

dync
www.dynamicscompanions.com
Dynamics Companions

- 117 -

www.blindsquirrelpublishing.com
© 2019 Blind Squirrel Publishing, LLC , All Rights Reserved

Confirming the Purchase Order

Once the Purchase order has been created, we will want to confirm the purchase order and send it to the vendor so that they can procure the items for us and deliver them to the store.

How to do it...

Step 1: Select PURCHASE action group and click on the Confirm button

To do this, we just want to confirm the purchase order.

To do this just select the **PURCHASE** action group and click on the **Confirm** button.

This will start the purchase order confirmation process.

After a few seconds, the purchase order will be confirmed, and we are done.

dync
www.dynamicscompanions.com
Dynamics Companions

- 118 -

www.blindsquirrelpublishing.com
© 2019 Blind Squirrel Publishing, LLC, All Rights Reserved

BLIND SQUIRREL
PUBLISHING

Confirming the Purchase Order

How to do it...

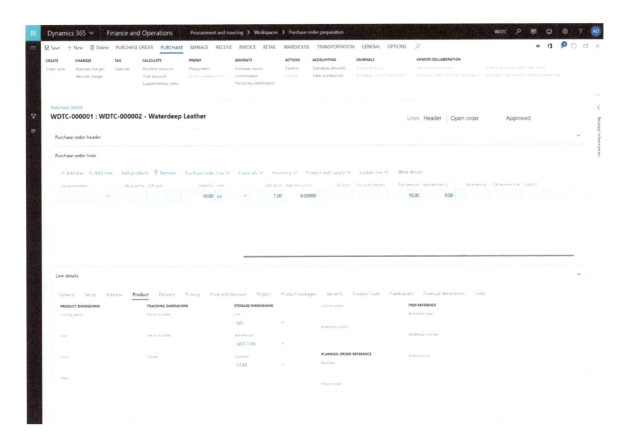

Step 1: Select PURCHASE action group and click on the Confirm button

To do this, we just want to confirm the purchase order.

To do this just select the **PURCHASE** action group and click on the **Confirm** button.

Confirming the Purchase Order

How to do it...

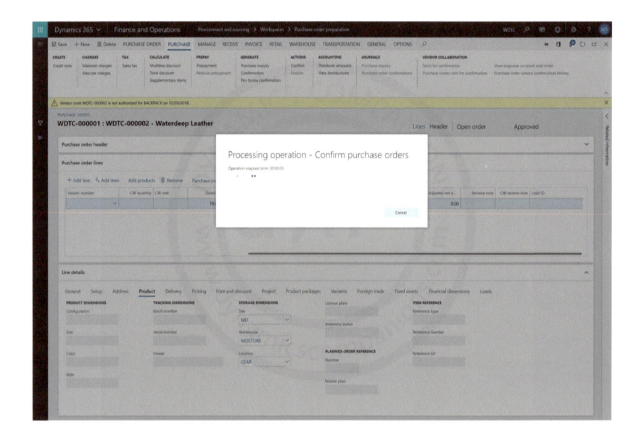

Step 1: Select PURCHASE action group and click on the Confirm button

This will start the purchase order confirmation process.

dync
www.dynamicscompanions.com
Dynamics Companions

- 120 -

www.blindsquirrelpublishing.com
© 2019 Blind Squirrel Publishing, LLC , All Rights Reserved

BLIND SQUIRREL
PUBLISHING

Confirming the Purchase Order

How to do it...

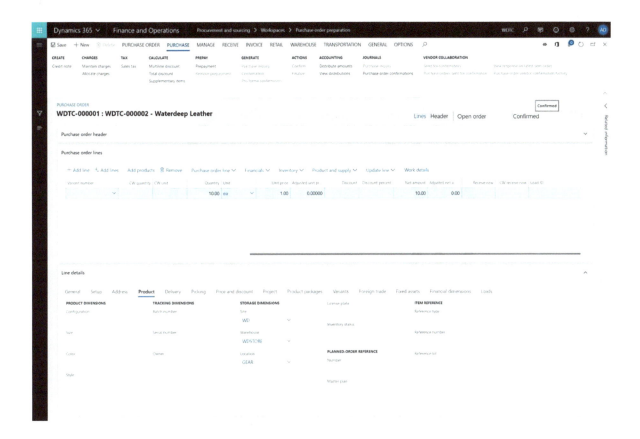

Step 1: Select PURCHASE action group and click on the Confirm button

After a few seconds, the purchase order will be confirmed, and we are done.

dync
dynamics companion

www.dynamicscompanions.com
Dynamics Companions

- 121 -

www.blindsquirrelpublishing.com
© 2019 Blind Squirrel Publishing, LLC , All Rights Reserved

BLIND SQUIRREL
PUBLISHING

Review

Congratulations. We have just created our first purchase order in the system and sent it off to the vendor to be fulfilled.

www.dynamicscompanions.com
Dynamics Companions

- 122 -

www.blindsquirrelpublishing.com
© 2019 Blind Squirrel Publishing, LLC , All Rights Reserved

BLIND SQUIRREL
PUBLISHING

Receiving Purchase Orders Into Inventory

When the vendor ships us the product, we will want to receive the product into inventory and confirm that what we ordered was what we asked for.

Topics Covered

- Creating a Purchase Order receipt

- Viewing the Product receipt journals

Creating a Purchase Order receipt

We can create the purchase receipt directly from the purchase order if we like.

How to do it...

Step 1: Expand Receive action bar and click on the Product receipt button

To do this, all we need to do is expand the **Receive** action bar and click on the **Product receipt** button.

This will open up the **Posting product receipt** panel where we can specify the receipt details.

Step 2: Update the Product receipt

We will start off by entering the receipt identification from the **Waterdeep Leather** company.

To do this, we will just need to update the **Product receipt** value.

This time, we will want to set the **Product receipt** to **1**.

Step 3: Expand Lines tab and click on the OK button

Also, we can change the receipt details at the line level as well before confirming the receipt.

To do this just expand the **Lines** tab and click on the **OK** button.

This will start off the receipt confirmation process.

Shortly after that, the product receipt should be processed, and the products will be received into inventory.

Creating a Purchase Order receipt

How to do it...

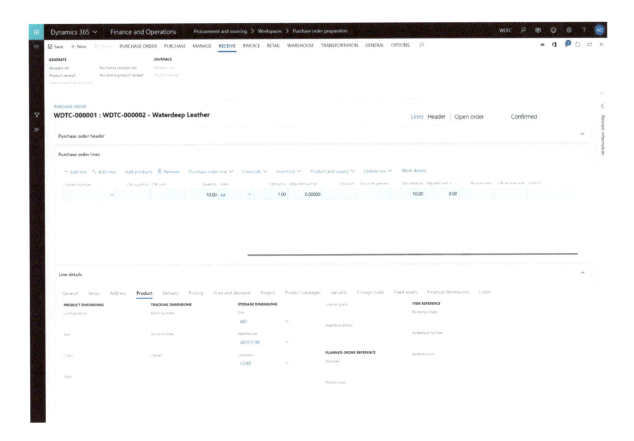

Step 1: Expand Receive action bar and click on the Product receipt button

To do this, all we need to do is expand the **Receive** action bar and click on the **Product receipt** button.

dync
www.dynamicscompanions.com
Dynamics Companions

- 125 -

www.blindsquirrelpublishing.com
© 2019 Blind Squirrel Publishing, LLC , All Rights Reserved

BLIND SQUIRREL
PUBLISHING

Creating a Purchase Order receipt

How to do it...

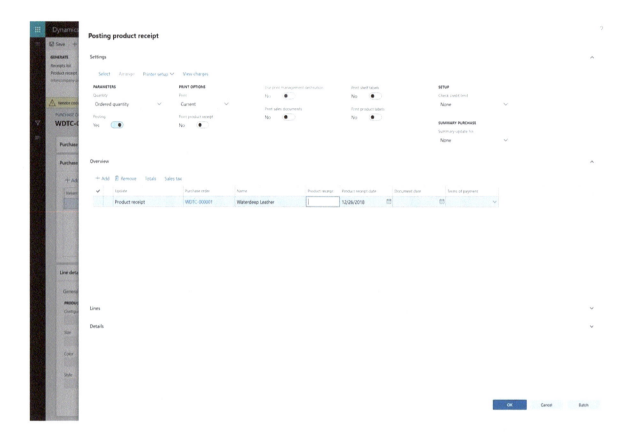

Step 1: Expand Receive action bar and click on the Product receipt button

This will open up the **Posting product receipt** panel where we can specify the receipt details.

Creating a Purchase Order receipt

How to do it...

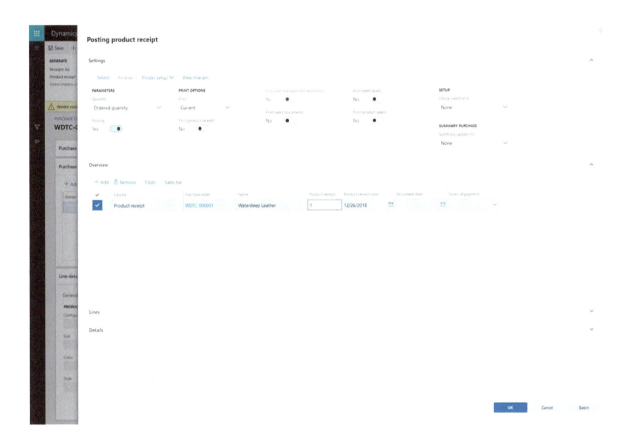

Step 2: Update the Product receipt

We will start off by entering the receipt identification from the **Waterdeep Leather** company.

To do this, we will just need to update the **Product receipt** value.

This time, we will want to set the **Product receipt** to **1**.

www.dynamicscompanions.com
Dynamics Companions

- 127 -

www.blindsquirrelpublishing.com
© 2019 Blind Squirrel Publishing, LLC , All Rights Reserved

BLIND SQUIRREL PUBLISHING

Creating a Purchase Order receipt

How to do it...

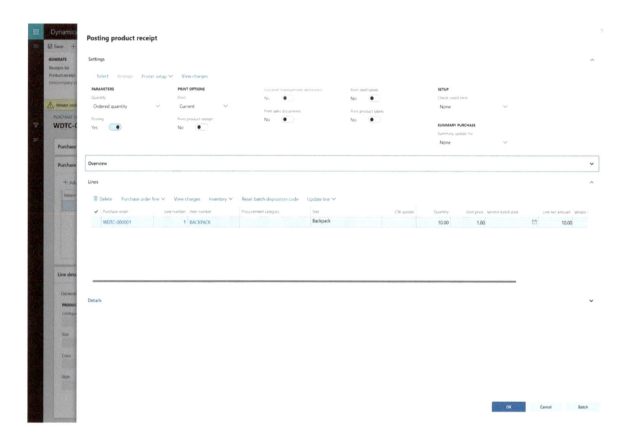

Step 3: Expand Lines tab and click on the OK button

Also, we can change the receipt details at the line level as well before confirming the receipt.

To do this just expand the **Lines** tab and click on the **OK** button.

www.dynamicscompanions.com
Dynamics Companions

- 128 -

www.blindsquirrelpublishing.com
© 2019 Blind Squirrel Publishing, LLC , All Rights Reserved

BLIND SQUIRREL
PUBLISHING

Creating a Purchase Order receipt

How to do it...

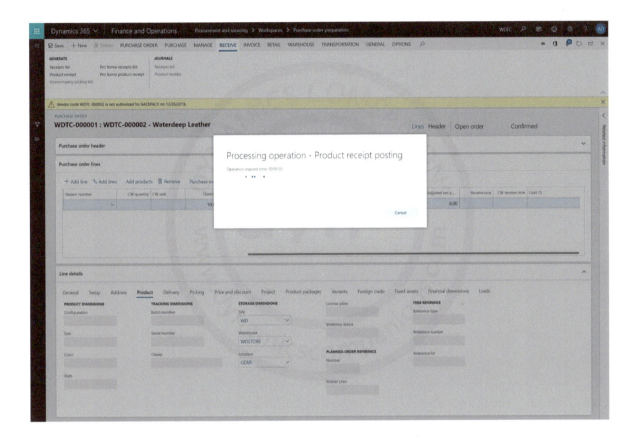

Step 3: Expand Lines tab and click on the OK button

This will start off the receipt confirmation process.

dync
dynamics companions

www.dynamicscompanions.com
Dynamics Companions

- 129 -

www.blindsquirrelpublishing.com
© 2019 Blind Squirrel Publishing, LLC , All Rights Reserved

BLIND SQUIRREL
PUBLISHING

Creating a Purchase Order receipt

How to do it...

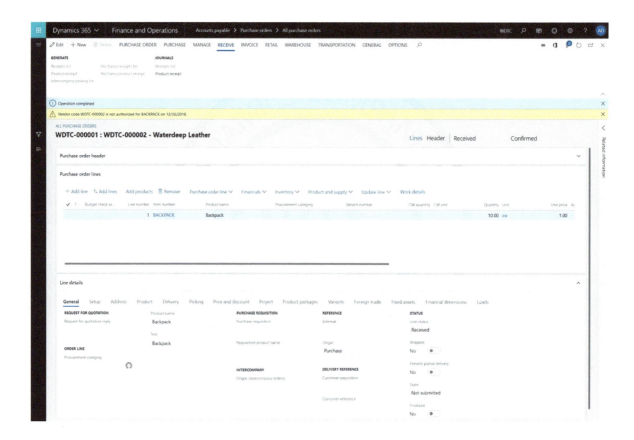

Step 3: Expand Lines tab and click on the OK button

Shortly after that, the product receipt should be processed, and the products will be received into inventory.

dync
dynamics companions

www.dynamicscompanions.com
Dynamics Companions

- 130 -

www.blindsquirrelpublishing.com
© 2019 Blind Squirrel Publishing, LLC , All Rights Reserved

BLIND SQUIRREL
PUBLISHING

Viewing the Product receipt journals

If we want to see more information about the product receipt, then we can always access the receipt journals that were created by the product receipt.

How to do it...

Step 1: Click on the Product receipts button

To do this, we just select the product receipts option.

To do this just click on the **Product receipts** button.

Step 2: Click on the View accounting button

This will list out all of the product receipts that have been associated with the purchase order.

If we want we can also drill into the financial details of the receipt.

To do this just click on the **View accounting** button.

This will show us all of the postings that were made by this one product receipt.

Viewing the Product receipt journals

How to do it...

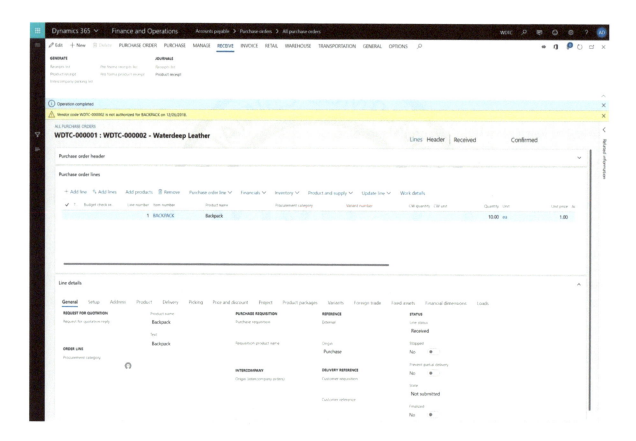

Step 1: Click on the Product receipts button

To do this, we just select the product receipts option.

To do this just click on the **Product receipts** button.

dync
dynamics companions

www.dynamicscompanions.com
Dynamics Companions

- 132 -

www.blindsquirrelpublishing.com
© 2019 Blind Squirrel Publishing, LLC , All Rights Reserved

BLIND SQUIRREL
PUBLISHING

Viewing the Product receipt journals

How to do it...

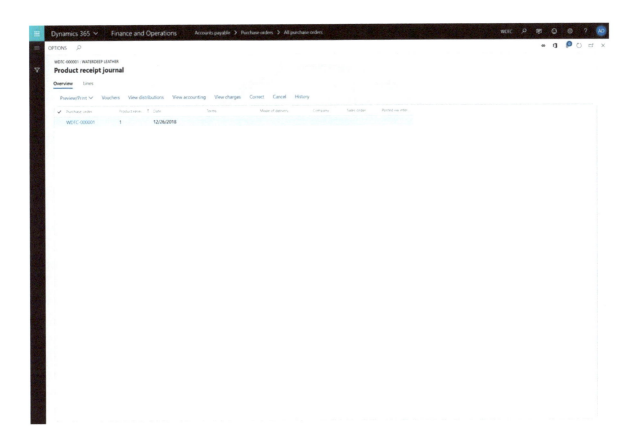

Step 2: Click on the View accounting button

This will list out all of the product receipts that have been associated with the purchase order. If we want we can also drill into the financial details of the receipt.

To do this just click on the **View accounting** button.

www.dynamicscompanions.com
Dynamics Companions

- 133 -

www.blindsquirrelpublishing.com
© 2019 Blind Squirrel Publishing, LLC , All Rights Reserved

BLIND SQUIRREL
PUBLISHING

Viewing the Product receipt journals

How to do it...

Step 2: Click on the View accounting button

This will show us all of the postings that were made by this one product receipt.

dync
www.dynamicscompanions.com
Dynamics Companions

- 134 -

www.blindsquirrelpublishing.com
© 2019 Blind Squirrel Publishing, LLC , All Rights Reserved

BLIND SQUIRREL
PUBLISHING

Review

Congratulations. We have now received in the products from the vendor and have all of the financial postings being made automatically for us in the background.

Viewing the Inventory On Hand

The final thing that we will do in this process is to take a quick look at the inventory that we now have on hand and we should be able to see the 10 backpacks that we received in.

Topics Covered

- Opening the Inventory On-Hand list inquiry

- Viewing the on-hand inventory

dync
www.dynamicscompanions.com
Dynamics Companions

- 136 -

www.blindsquirrelpublishing.com
© 2019 Blind Squirrel Publishing, LLC, All Rights Reserved

BLIND SQUIRREL
PUBLISHING

Opening the Inventory On-Hand list inquiry

To do this we will want to open up the **Inventory on-hand** inquiry.

How to do it...

Step 1: Open the On-hand list form through the menu search

Another way that we can find the **On-hand list** form is through the menu search feature.

We can do this by clicking on the search icon in the header of the form (or by pressing **ALT+G**)

and then type in **on-hand list** into the search box. Then you will be able to select the **On-hand list** form from the dropdown list.

This will open up the **On-hand inventory** inquiry form where we will be able to inquire on the inventory.

Opening the Inventory On-Hand list inquiry

How to do it...

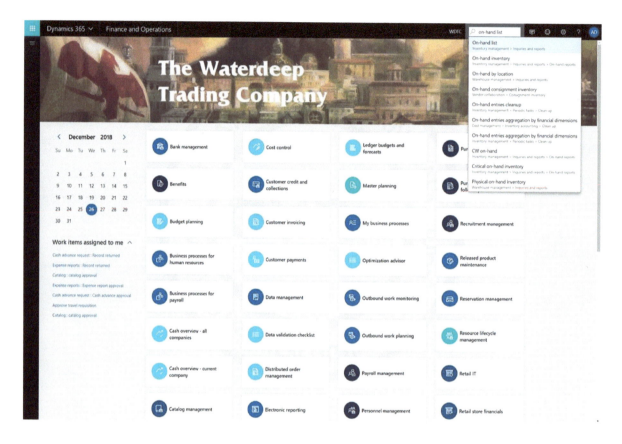

Step 1: Open the On-hand list form through the menu search

Another way that we can find the **On-hand list** form is through the menu search feature.

We can do this by clicking on the search icon in the header of the form (or by pressing **ALT+G**) and then type in **on-hand list** into the search box. Then you will be able to select the **On-hand list** form from the dropdown list.

dync
www.dynamicscompanions.com
Dynamics Companions

- 138 -

www.blindsquirrelpublishing.com
© 2019 Blind Squirrel Publishing, LLC , All Rights Reserved

BLIND SQUIRREL
PUBLISHING

Opening the Inventory On-Hand list inquiry

How to do it...

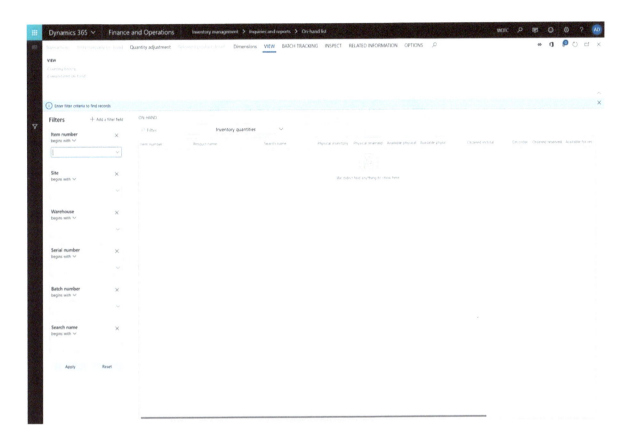

Step 1: Open the On-hand list form through the menu search

This will open up the **On-hand inventory** inquiry form where we will be able to inquire on the inventory.

Viewing the on-hand inventory

All we need to do now is do a search on the inventory.

How to do it...

Step 1: Click on the Apply button

We can filter out the inventory that we are looking for, although since we should only have one product in the store right now, we don't have to filter the results and can just inquire on everything.

To do this just click on the **Apply** button.

Now we will see that we have 10 backpacks in stock and ready to sell.

www.dynamicscompanions.com
Dynamics Companions

- 140 -

www.blindsquirrelpublishing.com
© 2019 Blind Squirrel Publishing, LLC, All Rights Reserved

BLIND SQUIRREL
PUBLISHING

Viewing the on-hand inventory

How to do it...

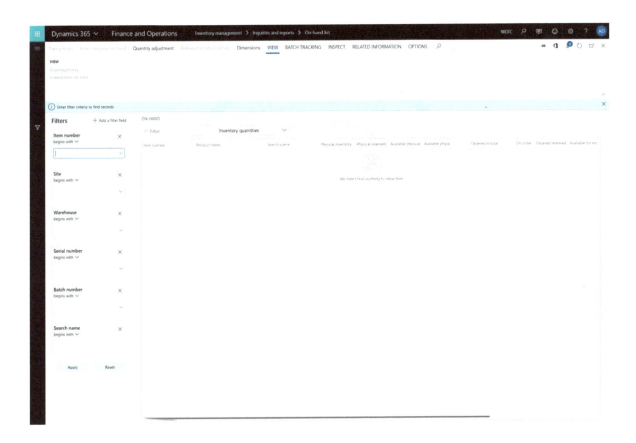

Step 1: Click on the Apply button

We can filter out the inventory that we are looking for, although since we should only have one product in the store right now, we don't have to filter the results and can just inquire on everything.

To do this just click on the **Apply** button.

www.dynamicscompanions.com
Dynamics Companions

- 141 -

www.blindsquirrelpublishing.com
© 2019 Blind Squirrel Publishing, LLC , All Rights Reserved

BLIND SQUIRREL
PUBLISHING

Viewing the on-hand inventory

How to do it...

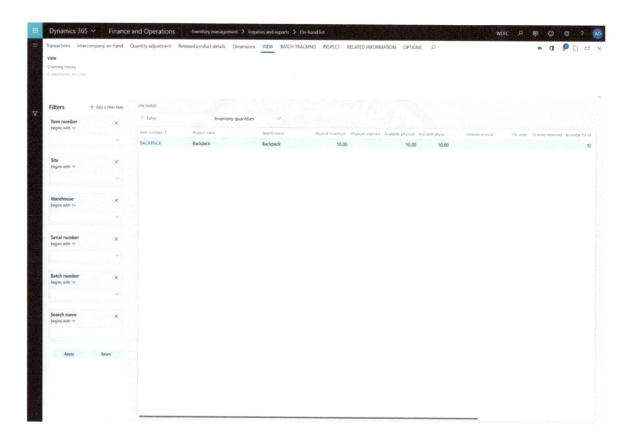

Step 1: Click on the Apply button

Now we will see that we have 10 backpacks in stock and ready to sell.

dync
Dynamics Companions
www.dynamicscompanions.com
Dynamics Companions

- 142 -

www.blindsquirrelpublishing.com
© 2019 Blind Squirrel Publishing, LLC , All Rights Reserved

BLIND SQUIRREL
PUBLISHING

Review

How easy was that? Now we are tracking all of the purchased inventory within the **Waterdeep Trading Company Store,** and we can keep a pulse on the inventory levels.

Summary

Congratulations. We have now purchased products from a vendor and received it into the store so that we can track the inventory levels.

Conclusion

In this module we have done quite a bit, including the configuration of the purchasing posting profiles and configurations, the setup and grouping of vendors, and also the creation, confirmation, and receipt of the purchase orders resulting in the tracking of the stock of inventory within the warehouse.

That is huge!

Now that we have all this product laying around, we had better start selling it.

About The Author

Murray Fife is an Author of over 25 books on Microsoft Dynamics including the Bare Bones Configuration Guide series of over 15 books which step the user through the setup of initial Dynamics instance, then through the Financial modules and then through the configuration of the more specialized modules like production, service management, and project accounting. You can find all his books on Amazon at **www.amazon.com/author/murrayfife**.

For more information on Murray, here is his contact information:

If you are interested in contacting Murray or want to follow his blogs and posts then here is all of his contact information:

Email: murray@murrayfife.com

Twitter: @murrayfife

Facebook: faceook.com/murraycfife

Google: google.com/+murrayfife

LinkedIn: linkedin.com/in/murrayfife

Blog: atinkerersnotebook.com

SlideShare: slideshare.net/murrayfife

Amazon: amazon.com/author/murrayfife

dync
www.dynamicscompanions.com
Dynamics Companions

- 146 -

www.blindsquirrelpublishing.com
© 2019 Blind Squirrel Publishing, LLC , All Rights Reserved

BLIND SQUIRREL
PUBLISHING